THERE

AND WELCOME TO

karlssonwilker inc.'s
TELLMEWHY
The First 24 Months of a New York Design Company

Published by Princeton Architectural Press
37 East Seventh Street
New York, New York 10003

For a free catalog of books, call 1.800.722.6657
Visit our web site at www.papress.com

Printed and bound in China

06 05 04 03 5 4 3 2 1 First edition

Project editing: Clare Jacobson
Copy editing: Mark Lamster
Book design: karlssonwilker inc., nyc

Library of Congress Cataloging-in-Publication Data

Jacobson, Clare, 1965-
karlssonwilker inc.'s tellmewhy : the first 24 months of a New York
design company / foreword by Stefan Sagmeister ; story written by
Clare Jacobson.– 1st ed.
p. cm.
ISBN 1-56898-416-2 (alk. paper)
1. Karlssonwilker Inc. 2. Karlsson, Hjalti. 3. Wilker, Jan.
4. Commercial art–New York (State)–New York–History–21st century.
5. Graphic arts–New York (State)–New York–History–21st century.
I. Title: Karlssonwilker inc.'s tell me why. II. Title.
NC999.4.K37J33 2003
741.6'092'2–dc21
2003009000

FOREWORD

I know Hjalti Karlsson and Jan Wilker. They both worked in my studio at one time. You can switch their names around with very pleasing results: Jan Karlsson and Hjalti Wilker. One of them is from Germany and the other one is from Iceland. Wilker is with no "s" at the end. If Jan would have been from Iceland, his last name would be Friedrichson, since if it's a boy in Iceland they always take Dad's first name and hang a "son" behind it. I, just for example, would too be called Karlsson on account of my papa Karl. I do not know what Hjalti's last name would be, if he would be from Germany, but am positive it would be rather hilarious.

Let me not forget to talk about Hjalti's and Jan's fantasticness: I think they are very fantastic. I don't just say that because this is a foreword and I better have something good to say about their designs, but because I really think they are fantastic: Fantastic design is when there are fantastic ideas developed in fantastic form, executed in fantastic style for fantastic reasons. Well, maybe their style is not so fantastic but just good and their reasons might only be so-so, but that still adds up to fantastic overall, thank you.

Before Jan finished art school in Stuttgart he moved to New York and opened a design studio with Hjalti and subsequently made the opening of a design studio with Hjalti in New York the subject of his final diploma in art school. Clever.

Hjalti is calm under stress but bites fingernails. This is a schizophrenic phenomenon common to Icelanders. When I asked somebody in Reykjavik about the reasons for the current proficiency of excellent Icelandic design, the answer was, "No history." Apparently Iceland did not have a word for design until the 1950s, and this allowed for a fresh start without being held back by historic baggage. However, there is a word for design in Germany in the 50s: "Das ist eine Hundefurz."

Hjalti and Jan are nice.

Stefan Sagmeister, New York 2002

INTRODUCTION

We started our company, karlssonwilker inc., in late 2000. We scraped up the few dollars we owned and the many ones we borrowed from our parents. We had one client. We set up an office on Sixth Avenue. And since we hardly knew each other at the time, we had no clue what would happen.

In this book we try to tell the story of our studio in its first two years in business. We show every single project we did, whether it was for a high-paying, low-paying, or non-paying client, or whether the clients were our fathers. In retrospect, some of the work makes us happy, some embarrassed.

We did not want the text to be solely about design, but also about other issues we had to deal with as brand-new business owners. Clare Jacobson, who wrote the story, spent many weekends and evenings with us in our office. She scribbled down notes, and her hands often got tired. We tried to keep the stories as we experienced them, and not as we would like them to have happened.

This book was designed in four weeks. The result is incomplete and callow, and it should be incomplete and callow. After two years in business, we are far from perfect.

Jan Wilker and Hjalti Karlsson
karlssonwilker inc.
New York City, May 2003

STORY

by Clare Jacobson

Prologue.

This story begins before karlssonwilker inc. begins, when karlsson is still Karlsson and wilker just Wilker.

Hjalti Karlsson grows up in Reykjavik, Iceland, where he studies physics at college. Encouraged by his mother, a recreational painter, he works the other side of his brain at some evening life-drawing classes, then redirects his studies to the Reykjavik School of Visual Art.

Waiting for his next bit of inspiration, he takes a job distributing candy. Then one day, after dropping off a case of M&Ms, he plays a scratch-off lottery ticket on a lark and wins $13,000. He decides to take this prize (along with some help from his parents) and move to New York to enroll in the Parsons School of Design. After receiving his degree in graphic design, he spends a year and a half at *Longevity*, working on the mature-women's magazine while his officemates work on *Penthouse*, then three years freelancing for Knoll, MoMA, Arnell Group, and the like. In September 1996, he gets a job with New York–based graphic designer Stefan Sagmeister, who becomes the official matchmaker/mentor of karlssonwilker.

In the meantime, Jan Wilker grows up in Ulm, Germany. He studies the flute for thirteen years, playing in various ensembles. At the age of twenty-one, after completing his mandatory fifteen months in the German civil service (an alternative to the army), he cofounds a creative studio called "buero fuer alles kreaktive & verrueckte" with a friend. They set up a typewriter, a copy machine, and a drawing board in an empty apartment in the hills overlooking Ulm, and fool around with design. Eventually they work on jobs for people with whom they grew up, and even collaborate with New York architect Richard Meier. Jan simultaneously cofounds another small enterprise, a surfing apparel company called Sharksucker, where he and two friends design and print T-shirts, among other things. Two years later, in 1995, he enrolls in the Technical University of Stuttgart to study architecture. He soon switches to graphic design at the State Academy of Fine Arts, Stuttgart, from where he applies for an internship with Sagmeister.

Both Hjalti and Jan discover Stefan (to whom, like most everyone else, they refer by his first name) through his designs for CDs—Hjalti sees H. P. Zinker's *Mountains of Madness*, and Jan Pat Metheny's *Imaginary Days*. He is the only designer with whom they want to work; it is Stefan or no one. Hjalti arrives first—his three-month trial job has already lasted three years when Jan comes calling. That first call is not the kind of introduction that typically sets off a partnership. Jan phones Stefan's office expecting to address the Austrian in comfortable German. When Hjalti answers the phone instead, Jan is thrown off guard. He fumbles with his high-school English and manages only to blurt out, "Well, Sagmeister, is he, eh, okay?" Hjalti is as confused as Jan, and both hang up shaking their heads.

When Jan does arrive, after a more fluent conversation with Stefan, he and Hjalti find they have a lot in common. They are both young—Hjalti is just thirty-two and Jan just twenty-seven when they meet—and good-looking. They have similar tastes in music, clothes, and food. They both have a "j" pronounced like a "y" in their names, which always confuses Americans. And they share a similar design sense. They take their work seriously but know design can be fun. Graphic design is not their first love but a design sense is almost inbred in them. Yet somehow their similarities do not make them fast friends. They hesitate to socialize with each other outside of the office and stay in their separate worlds.

After three months at Stefan's studio, Jan returns to Stuttgart to get back to his studies. Hjalti has seen many of Stefan's interns come and go, but when Jan leaves, Hjalti keeps in touch via email. A quick "How are you?" one day is followed by "Fine, and you?" two days later. But from somewhere within these short emails the two decide to start a business together. Hjalti claims it was Jan's idea; Jan claims it was Hjalti's. They both now agree that they would not have joined with any other person, though they know how saccharine that sounds.

 The timing for their new venture seems predestined. Hjalti has been looking for a change, and when Stefan decides to take a year-long sabbatical from his heavy design routine, the time is right. Hjalti will stay with his mentor until July 2000 to work on Stefan's monograph, *Made You Look*, but then he will be free for his new pursuit. Jan is ready to join him except for the small matter of finishing his master's degree. When he convinces his professors that "I open a design studio in New York" is a valid thesis topic, he, too, is ready for the new studio. The partners-to-be are rather casual about starting a business. Neither is too excited or too nervous making such a serious commitment with someone he does not know very well. They feel confident, just happy that something different is happening in their lives. It helps that they are both newly in love, with all the confidence and happiness that brings.

 They have good instincts. Their acquaintance easily blossoms into a relationship more like that of siblings than business partners. Hjalti assumes the role of the older, more serious brother who is simultaneously trying to keep the younger, more rascally brother in check while holding back his guffaws at his antics. But sometimes Hjalti gets silly and Jan gets morose. They have a knack for playing off each other and easily become good friends.

 They may be inseparable, but they are not indistinguishable. Hjalti is blonde; Jan is tall. Hjalti has the voice of a disc jockey; Jan has a tattoo on his lower back. When they drink too much, Hjalti is more likely to touch people he does not know, while Jan tends to act up. Hjalti is reserved, quietly clever, and fond of saying "super," as in "super good," "super bad," and "super excellent." Jan is well read, politically minded, and fond of lewd discussions. Theirs is a combination that works. And sometimes does not work. But it is a story worth telling.

Getting Started.

Hjalti and Jan know that setting up an office requires much more than an emailed handshake. They have worked long enough to understand the importance of an office's identity. (Fortunately, they have not worked long enough to actually use that nasty word in a conversation.) The first decision for their new partnership is its name. The duo briefly considers "rocket," but settles on "karlssonwilker" via email. These emails are long gone, but they might have read something like this:

hey, mr. germany,
how's life treating you in your homeland?
and how's love life?
we're still working on the book here.
but we should be done in a few weeks.
what about our little enterprise here?
any thoughts?
h

hello, icelander
i told you i'm ready.
but rocket doesn't really fly.
karlssonwilker,
Karlsson & Wilker?
Karlsson Wilker?
Karlwil, karlsker grafik studio?
tell me.
and say hello to stefan.
jan

wilkerkarlsson,
Wilker-Karlsson,
hjalnti, hjan, hj-design?
stefan says hello.
h

karlssonwilker just sounds better, sadly...
so i'll be always second from now on.
jan

karlssonwilker inc. it is then.
i wouldn't know anything else.
h

Next Hjalti searches for karlssonwilker inc.'s home in the city while Jan sends his virtual support from Germany. In June 2000, at the height of New York's real-estate boom, an agent shows Hjalti thirty office spaces, one more unacceptable than the next. He sees a cockroach-infested hole followed by a dorm-sized hovel followed by a windowless hell. Finally he discovers a dream space, one of those large, bright, conveniently located places with rent so low even its landlord is surprised to learn its asking price.

The office that gets "karlssonwilker inc." on its door is on the third floor of a four-story walk-up on Sixth Avenue just above Fourteenth Street, a part of town not typically considered a design center. The neighborhood is better known for its cheap and easy merchandise—a clothing store advertising "every item $10" across from a guy selling $10 luggage on the street. Hjalti looks out the window at the Funny Cry Happy Gift Shop next to Valentino Jewelry, both vying for attention with faded awnings and outdated window displays. There is a Dunkin' Donuts on the ground floor of the new office, a McDonald's across the street, and a KFC around the corner; Hjalti and Jan will use them all well.

Their new home selected, Hjalti and Jan set up their virtual home. They work on it together via email and launch www.karlssonwilker.com in July 2000. The site has a simple message on its only page: "we do design," set in Courier. As the unborn office has no design work to display, the site instead uses the stuttering "Fred" voice of the Mac OS to announce karlssonwilker's opening:

Test test test 1, 2, 3, ttt, ttttt, yo yo what's up what's up, vicinity, ok, now, lets go. karlsson-wilker inc. has been formed. We are glad to be open for public now, by the way, we are in new york city! This website is under construction and will present a new design company with a new name, and hom hek k kkk lo lolalalala, no, aha, aaarerararararaerererer, eh! Shit, whatever, but by the way, we are in new york city, 5, 3, 6, avenue 6, new york new york, 1, 0, 0, 1, 1, you can reach us under, 2, 1, 2, 9, 2, 9, 8, 0, 6, 4, the fax number is, 2, 1, 2, 9, 2, 9, 8, 0, 6, 3. you know what? They will ra, ra, rock the place, yeah! so thanks for stopping by and come back again soon, bye bye and say hello to your mom.

Then an email address appears on the screen, showmethemeaningofbeinglonely@karlsson-wilker.com, a name copied from the title of a Backstreet Boys song. When they try to register this address they find out it has too many characters. So they change it to tellmewhy@karlssonwilker.com, borrowing from the Backstreet Boys' "I Want It That Way." They will share a memorable night or two singing this song at a downtown karaoke bar.

Jan arrives from Germany with only a red Wilson tennis bag stuffed with clothes, a male version of Heidi come to start his new life. He has no work visa, but only a three-month tourist visa. His girlfriend, Ella Smolarz, remains in Germany; she will join him in three weeks. He has no place to live, so he moves into Hjalti's place on the Upper West Side while Hjalti stays with his girlfriend, Vera Yuan, in her West Village apartment. Jan's absent visa, girlfriend, and apartment are not ideal, but these are not things to worry about—Hjalti and Jan have an office! A light-filled, Website-filled, Dunkin' Donut–filled office! The celebrants buy a couple of six-packs and head for Central Park.

Back on Sixth Avenue, the pair continues to set up karlssonwilker. They consider designing a logo but are hesitant to do so; people often judge a company by its logo, and the team does not know what they want to be just yet. So they simply print their name in Trade Gothic Bold (or, at other times, in Din—they are not too exacting) to make a letterhead. It seems like non-design at the time, but they have to admit that even a non-design is a design. Setting their names as one word is a design choice, as is setting them in lower case. Each small decision now defines karlssonwilker. Without a logo to drive the look of a letterhead, the partners focus on its content:

This is a LETTER
To:
Regarding:
Today is:
Yesterday was:
This playful text also suggests what the new office will become.

There is more than design to a design office, however. The partners sketch out various ideas for a business plan. One early version lists three items: six weeks holiday, five CD covers, and money. For the money part, they pool all that they have. Hjalti gathers $15,000 from his savings and a loan from his parents. Jan's matching deposit comes from his parents and his grandfather. Stefan encourages his pupils to make a budget and meet with his accountant, which they do. Hjalti even writes up a spreadsheet to balance their money against the studio's expected expenses. Reading this document two years later, it is almost laughable. There is $3,000 budgeted for two tables, $550 for a digital camera, and $100 a month for a cleaning service. In reality they spend $200 on three tables, never buy the digital camera, and clean their office themselves. For items like insurance, utilities, and taxes, there are just big question marks. They have slated $2,500 per month as salary for each partner and labeled it, "What is the minimum you can get by with in first months?" They will find that the minimum is much, much less.

Finally, they are ready to make their empty office a real studio. They start with three gifts from Stefan: a G3 PowerMac, a table, and a chair. Hjalti brings in an old monitor from home, and now karlssonwilker is ready to work. That is, Karlsson or Wilker is ready to work. So they write the first check on their joint account for a new i-Mac. They station it on the same single table by a window overlooking Sixth Avenue, where they work side by side, elbow to elbow. Here they share ideas and Chinese take-out and even an email address, tellmewhy@karlssonwilker.com.

In another month, they buy a third computer, a G4. They dedicate the i-Mac to their database and to Internet searches, and use the other two computers for design work. Hjalti takes the G4 and Jan the G3. But their computers do not become their private workstations, flanked by personal Post-its or photographs. Instead a project stays on one computer—whichever computer it started on—while the project makers trade back and forth to work on it.

Next they get an old sofa and a matching chair, some ashtrays for Jan's pack-and-a-half-a-day habit, and a $500 red Husky tool drawer, which becomes one of their prized possessions. They put in two phone lines for the calls they expect will soon be pouring in. Karlssonwilker is ready to work.

Really Getting Started.

Their first client arrives in September 2000 (the first of their twenty-four months, if you are counting). When Stefan takes his sabbatical, he directs jazz musician Pat Metheny to his protégés. For Hjalti, this is a simple enough transition. He and Stefan have worked with Pat on four CDs, including the *Trio 99–00* packaging that will serve as a basis for this new one. But for Jan, this is big. It was the design of Pat's *Imaginary Days* that drew his attention to Stefan's office, and now this same musician walks through the door as his first client. Pat's label, Warner Brothers, is also big, and the job pays $7,500.

Pat meets the designers at their new office to work on the *Trio–Live* packaging. Neither Hjalti nor Jan are devoted fans of his music, so neither are star-struck as they approach the meeting. And Pat puts them at ease. He is laid-back, as his T-shirt, short jeans shorts, white socks, and sneakers (atypical attire for a New Yorker) attest.

For his new CD, he has collected bundles of uncut tapes from months of international touring with his trio. At each new meeting with Hjalti and Jan, Pat has a new idea for how he will edit the CD. One week it is to be the most mellow, down-to-earth compilation, the next the weirdest live album ever. Each new cut calls for a change in the design, which Pat is eager to discuss. After each of the six meetings they share, he follows up with even more input via email. But karlssonwilker does not mind his vacillation and intervention. *Trio–Live* is the only work in the new office, and so they are happy to dedicate all their time to it.

They show Pat three design ideas. For this they unlearn one of Stefan's lessons: to show one design, *the* design, to the client. For the first design they cut out the letters in the title and set them up for a photo shoot on a sidewalk. It is a warm fall day, and the two partners happily spend it on the

20

street outside their office, Hjalti working the camera while Jan works the crowds. The resulting shot looks as if three-dimensional type is standing on a stage. A second design reuses the type style from *Trio 99–00* and expresses the trio as three materials: a sidewalk, a concrete floor, and a wood floor. The designers enjoy including photographs from their first office in their first design project.

The third proposal, the one used on the final package, is like the second, except the three materials are replaced by three simple color bands. Jan and Hjalti play with variations in yellow and blue, jumping from one scheme to another as fast as the computer allows before landing on a final plan of orange, blue, and dark gray. Karlssonwilker does not yet own a Pantone color-specifying book—one more item to add to their Husky—and so the partners choose the colors from their computer screen. As color is really the essential design element in the package, this may seem like a less-than-serious approach. Jan later admits the colors for the CD are "fairly random," while Hjalti claims, "colors are more for wallpaper." But at least one critic sees meaning in their choices. Pascal Paquette writes in an online review for Brandera.com:

> Music theory meets color theory on a contemporary jazz album that at first glance isn't very exciting. Yes, but dig a bit to understand the concept: in music, one sound layers on top of another. The album cover layers three stripes of color. Black at the bottom, a stable, solid color: the base guitar. Blue in the mid stripe, a cool, confident color: the bass guitar. The top stripe is an appetizing, vibrant, decorative orange: Pat Metheny's guitar and high-ends....The three-panel album opens to a solid dark teal interior: harmony, completion, comfort.

The designers are amused by this critique, but they are happy to accept it. They are even happier to accept credit for the art direction, design, and *ferlauffe* (incorrect German for "gradation") on the CD package. "Karlssonwilker inc." is now in print, and both Pat and Warner Brothers are pleased with the design.

Hjalti and Jan do not have a second client lined up. But a client does arrive, as many early clients do, as an acquaintance. Constantin Boym, a New York–based product designer, knows Hjalti through mutual friends. He has just designed two series of miniature souvenir buildings: "Buildings of Disaster" memorializes sites of tragic events, while "Missing Monuments" replicates famous buildings that never existed or no longer exist. He asks karlssonwilker to design a poster to promote the products as "Souvenirs for the End of the Century." From it, people will be able to order a copy of Three Mile Island, the Watergate Hotel, Newton's Cenotaph, or the Palace of the Soviets to display next to their miniatures of the Eiffel Tower and Big Ben.

Things start off a little rough for the three men. Though Constantin is comfortable with Hjalti, he is unsure about Jan. In the designers' first meeting with him, as in meetings with most clients early on, Hjalti does most of the talking, and Jan, uncertain about his English, keeps silent.

Since his first failed phone chat with Hjalti, he is anxious about speaking incorrectly. (One day he picks up the office phone to find someone asking for Jan Wilker, and he denies he is there—denies he is he—rather than struggles through the conversation.) This silence makes Constantin nervous. He thinks Jan is weird, and the feeling is mutual. Jan has a hard time understanding what Constantin is saying and how he is feeling.

When their client is out the door, Jan tells Hjalti that he does not want to work on a poster because he thinks it would waste paper. Instead, karlssonwilker should consider the environment and make a smaller piece. Jan is fresh from school, so he has confidence in the ability of his work to affect the world. Hjalti, overwhelmed by Jan's enthusiasm, agrees. Though the partners do not present their politics to Constantin, they do show him a proposal for a different kind of piece.

When Jan considers this proposal today, he remembers his call for environmental action as the "silliest thing I've ever said." In part, he is self-critical of his attempt to make design out to be more than it is. But primarily he is amused by his "environmentally friendly" solution—a four-page mailer printed on light board. Its paper content is greater than a poster's would have been, and it is finished with a less-than-friendly plastic laminate.

Despite this shaky start, the mailer progresses well. Hjalti and Jan create dynamic, exaggerated, three-dimensional type that plays well against the sober little souvenirs. Budget constraints force their original four-color proposal into two colors, but they do not object. As the souvenirs themselves are monochrome, it seems somehow appropriate. Still, the designers are not happy with the end result; the mailer is not printed well, and its layout is a bit awkward—at least to them. They display parts of it on their Website and in their portfolio, but they never show off the complete finished piece. Constantin never knows about their disappointment. He is pleased with the design, and will return to them with more work.

Two jobs in the first month of business—one for a major music label and one for a well-known product designer—are a good way to start a business. Hjalti and Jan are happy guys. They decide to treat their office to some new furniture—sharing one small table is fun for only so long. They spend a day driving to all the Home Depot stores in northern New Jersey looking for three matching, unscratched wood doors to use as table tops. They put so much mileage on their rented van that the U-Haul attendant cannot believe the odometer when they return it at day's end. But they have their table tops. They get three matching black leather chairs from a second-hand store on Twenty-fifth Street. They look good in front of the new tables, and are fun to roll around the office. Hjalti prints some small signs, perhaps inspired by their day on the road, and attaches them to the chair backs:

how am I designing?
call (212) 929 8064
safety is our goal
the new york city's karlssonwilker inc.

Hjalti's girlfriend brings karlssonwilker its third job. Vera works for the branding firm Landor, famous for updating the images of customers like FedEx. Landor hires outside designers to present proposals to their clients, and Vera hires her lover and his partner. The project is for Ginsana; it wants to update its packaging for an "all-natural energizer" called "Surge." This is difficult work for Hjalti. Coming from Stefan's studio, an office with clients like Lou Reed, David Byrne, and the Rolling Stones, he finds the work somewhat degrading. And it does not help that he is working for his girlfriend—and living in her apartment.

Jan has no issues about the work. For him Surge is pure fun. The work comes down to clicking through typefaces and patterning brightly colored yellow and green backgrounds, colors chosen by the client. A couple of days of this provides the studio a month's rent. Some of the proposals look more like laundry detergent boxes than herbal supplement packages, and some of the best are actually designed by Vera herself. None are picked up by Ginsana, which opts to vary its original design only slightly. Vera soon leaves her job, and so the Landor mine dries up. This is not to say she will stop bringing work to karlssonwilker.

One day at the end of October the office power is turned off, forcing Hjalti and Jan to shut down for the day. They move some folding chairs to the Sixth Avenue sidewalk to watch their busy neighborhood. When they see the garbage truck on its biweekly rounds, they turn and smile to each other. They have never signed up for garbage pickup, and instead buy trash bags that match Dunkin' Donut's bags and throw their things in with their neighbors' waste. It takes a little practice to get this just right—they hide their heavier trash in the middle of the bag and pad the outside with waste paper—but soon they have a system down. They figure they pay for the service with all the money they spend on their twice-a-day habit of coffee and donuts. And Hjalti and Jan daily endure the overpowering smells of cinnamon in the morning and something like stale cheese in the afternoon, which they bring home each night in their clothing. It is only fair.

October turns to November. Hjalti watches the leaves disappear as he walks from Vera's West Village apartment. Jan watches the tourists arrive as he takes the subway from Hjalti's apartment on the Upper West side. They meet on Fourteenth Street, where the discount shops are offering even bigger discounts for holiday sales, and greet their friend Constantin. He is still grinning with pleasure from their work on his souvenirs mailer, and he brings with him a recommendation to Vitra, the renowned manufacturer of high-end modern furniture. He has designed an exhibition for them and passes on his connection to karlssonwilker.

Hjalti and Jan know what a great client Vitra can be. The company has been an arbiter of good design for over fifty years, and an association with it could mean that karlssonwilker has truly arrived—only two months into their business. The partners see visions of a few swank tables replacing the doors-on-legs they use now. They eagerly put together a portfolio of their work on Pat's CD and Constantin's mailer, as well as a few solo pieces by Jan—some T-shirts, a poster, and a CD package for *No Eats Yes*, designed for the German bassist Hellmut Hattler. They present this work as individual pieces on individual boards, fattening up the packaging if not the content, and place it in a case Hjalti made eight years ago, when he first finished school and started looking for work.

Despite their enthusiasm, they keep themselves cool. Maybe too cool. The day they meet with the Vitra people, Hjalti does not shave and Jan wears the sweater and jeans he wore the day before. When they are presented the project—a new catalog to promote Vitra's furniture—they calmly answer questions and take their leave. They fax their bid a couple of days later and wait for the phone to ring. That should do it. But it does not. Designers are not hired on design alone. They learn this lesson a few weeks later when the woman who got the job attends one of their bimonthly office parties. She tells them how she phoned Vitra for months until they returned her call. Hjalti and Jan have not considered such salesmanship. They never tell their potential clients that they are the best people for the job, because they do not know that they are the best. They do know they could do good work for them. This time, they do not get that chance.

With little work and little prospect for more, karlssonwilker takes an improbable next step—they look for an intern. Jan had a good experience interning with Stefan; maybe he and Hjalti can offer the same joy to a student of their own. Or maybe they think that New York design offices are supposed to have interns. Maybe they just want to fill their third chair. Whatever the reason, they post an ad at Parsons School of Design (Hjalti's alma mater):

> this is an offer for an internship. we are happy to announce our brand new opening. we are a small design company and our name is karlssonwilker inc. we are located on 6th avenue between 14th and 15th street. mr. karlsson is super happy, because now he is his own boss after the last 4 years working with stefan sagmeister, who is always a happy guy. the other half of the company is happy in his own way, because now he is in new york, and not in europe anymore, although europe is not a bad place to be in, whatever, this is about an internship and not about the north america vs. europe topic. so if you are a happy guy or a happy girl, it's good for you. we only need an intern. bye bye and call 929-8064. this is an offer for an internship.

Five people reply, and Hjalti and Jan pick Allejandra Santos to come in a couple of days each week. This will cost them only lunch and subway fare, as New York design interns are used to working for the glory of it. The partners are uncomfortable sending Allejandra to the post office or making her sort papers, and so instead give her the best of the little design work they have. But still they find that their protégée, far from enjoying the freedom of working a few days on a single project, craves direction and attention. She is used to specific design projects and daily critiques, not open-programmed, open-ended work. Hjalti and Jan have no desire to play professor, so theirs is not such a joyful story after all. At the end of January, Allejandra tells her bosses that they really do not need an intern.

Hjalti and Jan celebrate three months in business by having some friends over for a party. The invitations go out via email, with the same tag line they always do, "Hello everyone! Once again you are happily invited to an evening with real people." The office transforms into a room packed with these "real people," mainly graphic designers. A guy from Nickelodeon drops in on the recommendation of a friend, starts up a conversation with the partners, and asks to look at a display of their work. He assumes that this design office party, like others he has attended, is set up to promote the business. But Jan and Hjalti never think of selling themselves in the middle of their fun. And, even if they wanted to schmooze, they do not have business cards. So while they are drinking beer and dancing the limbo to Ricky Martin's "Livin' la Vida Loca"—Allejandra is especially good at this—their friends are passing out their own cards and picking up potential clients.

Despite their attitude, or maybe because of it, the Nickelodeon guy invites them up to his office to show him their work. He schedules a one o'clock meeting, but Hjalti and Jan, oblivious to the time, leave their office at ten past. Nickelodeon is just thirty blocks north of their office, so this should not be too much of a problem. But the traffic on Sixth Avenue is horrible, and they cannot find a cab. They do not have a cell phone with them, and so have no way of telling him they will be late. They finally arrive at half past two, and apologetically present their work. Not surprisingly, he never calls them for a job.

November marks the end of Jan's allotted stay in the States, so he and Hjalti visit a lawyer to apply for a work visa. Hjalti has some sense of this from his own experience getting a green card a few years back. He assumes it will be a simple enough procedure. But the lawyer tells them karlssonwilker is too small to sponsor Jan, and having Jan's name in the company presents an additional problem. He can start working on getting a visa, but for now Jan will have to return to Germany with Ella.

Before he goes, Hjalti and Jan meet with their accountant, who insists that they set up a formal agreement for karlssonwilker. He tells them horror stories of partnerships gone sour, of friends turned into enemies over money. Though the pair believe this can never happen to them, they sign a simple letter:

Agreement between Hjalti Karlsson and Jan Wilker. This is to certify that Mr. Hjalti Karlsson and Mr. Jan Wilker are part owners of karlssonwilker inc., New York, located by the date of this contract at 536 6th Avenue, New York, NY 10011, U.S.A. $15,000 each were paid to found the company. All future payments or income will be divided into two halves.

(Two years later, when they are looking for this letter, they have a hard time finding it. Jan thinks his copy is somewhere in Germany; Hjalti eventually digs his out from the bottom of an unmarked file.)

With Jan off in Germany, Hjalti alone is responsible for finding the next job. He has some help from an old friend, Skúli Sverrisson, a bassist who has worked with Laurie Anderson, among others. Skúli introduces his fellow Icelander to Composer Recording Inc., a music label promoting contemporary American musicians like John Cage and Harry Partch. (Jan's brother has a handful of their albums in his collection.) Now CRI is launching an experimental jazz sublabel dubbed "Blueshift." Its proposed six to ten releases a year could mean some constant work for karlssonwilker.

Hjalti meets John Schultz, executive director of CRI, and Brian Conley, its production manager, to discuss the series. (Unlike Warner Brothers, Pat Metheny's label, CRI never includes its musicians in design discussions.) John wants a distinct look for Blueshift, something that will graphically unite his diverse artists. Hjalti (and Jan, via email) want to avoid a basic grid, a repeated font or color, or some other design system to distinguish the series, and instead create a uniquely identifiable production technique. They propose printing the liner of each CD in black and white, and hot-stamping or silk-screening the jewel case in a single color. Both methods are affordable, because of Blueshift's low production runs. (Their small numbers also means small pay—one-tenth of the Warner Brothers fee.) Hjalti shows CRI six possibilities for this system, ranging from an all-type treatment to graphic patterns to photographs.

The first Blueshift CD, *Sideshow: Songs of Charles Ives*, comes from vibraphonist and composer Matt Moran. Hjalti uses a stock photograph of a forest as the black-and-white background view (he realizes much later that he never charged CRI the $75 the studio paid for it) and stamps two blocks in bold red on the case. He and Jan alternate on the design of future Blueshift releases. They are excited to use it to experiment with a design series and they appreciate the creative freedom they have in it—this is one of the benefits of working for a small company like CRI.

Meanwhile, Jan is having a horrible stay in Germany. He spends most of his time on Ella's couch, drinking too much, smoking too much (accidentally lighting her sofa on fire one evening), and pining for his new office. Hjalti is also having a rough time. Karlssonwilker is empty without Jan, and the occasional company of Allejandra is not enough. He hopes some new clients can help fill his empty space and time. Story continues on page 65

So this is us in late 2000, trying to get our new entrepreneur looks down, and ready to go.

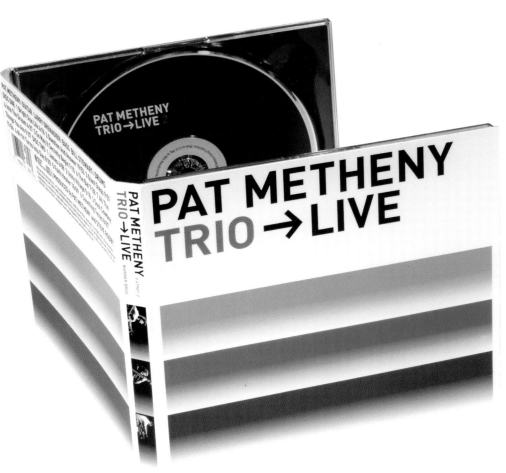

This was the very first job in our brand new studio, and our last for Mr. Metheny.
We did many, more or less random color variations. The final design was taken from a very early one. (20)

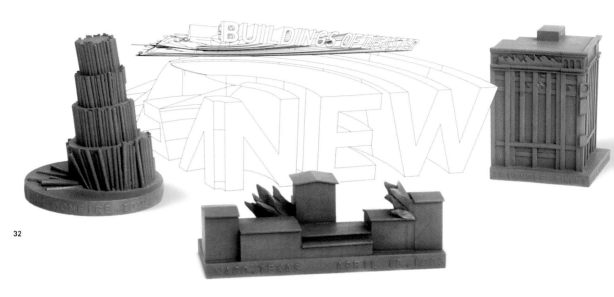

Design for "The End" catalog featuring Missing Monuments and Buildings of Disaster: destructed 3D type floating around, wrong perspectives. (21)

>>Two days of clicking through typefaces. The client, a branding company, called it "type exploration." (23)

EL WAITRESS

EL VIS

EL EVATOR

FRESHMANSOPHMOREJUNIORSENIOR5THYEARSENIORGRADSTUDENTEMPLOYEEPROFESSORHAPPYLONELYDEAD

BREAKFASTLUNCHDINNERBREAKFASTLUNCHDINNERBREAKFASTLUNCHDINNERBREAKFASTLUNCHDINNER

I'M YOUR DAD'S COMPUTER

CHOPSTICK THAT WRITES

EMPLOYEES MUST WASH THEIR OWN HANDS

HELP. IT'S DARK IN HERE.

LONG PILLOW FOR TINY PEOPLE.

CAPTURED HOURGLASS FUGITIVES.

THIS IS WHAT HAPPENS TO NAUGHTY LITTLE TREES

DENTISTS MAKE ON AVERAGE $120,000 A YEAR

EL MIKADO

Our first restaurant design, for a diner in Philadelphia, on a university campus.

38

EL FONT

ABCDEFGHIJKL
MNOPQRST
UVWXYZ
1234567890
$@&!?

EL DINER

SPEND MORE MONEY TO IMPROVE YOUR REPUTATION

3925 WALNUT STREET
PHILADELPHIA, PENNSYLVANIA
UNITED STATES OF AMERICA
T 215-735-2955

YES. WE'RE OPEN.

NEXT TIME BRING YOUR FRIENDS

EL DINER

TWENTYFOUR OURS.

EL DINER

EFFICIENT FOOD.

The El Font typeface and one color did the job. Silly lines for silly students.

Sadly, the diner closed down after only 3 months in business. (65)

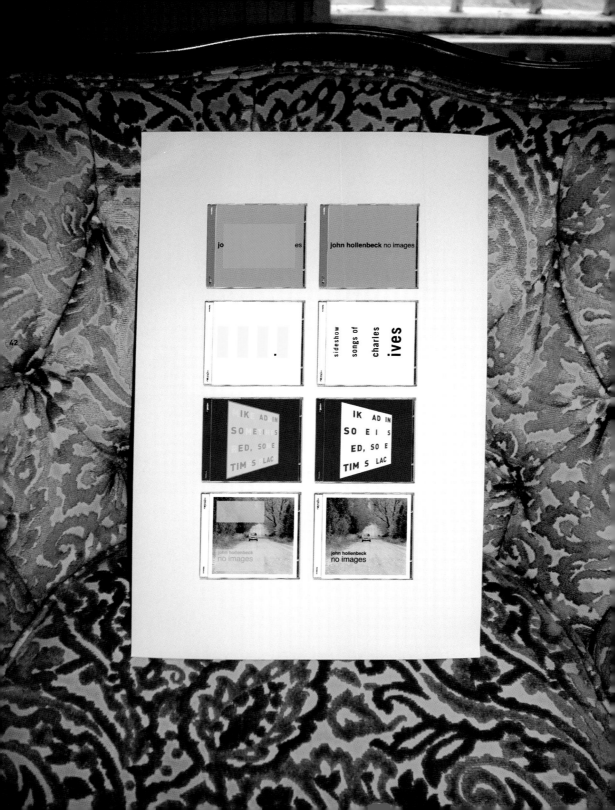

This was the first release of the newly founded CRI/Blueshift series.

<This is the old presentation board we used to show the design idea to the client: all CDs are silkscreened with one color onto jewel cases with b/w interiors. (26)

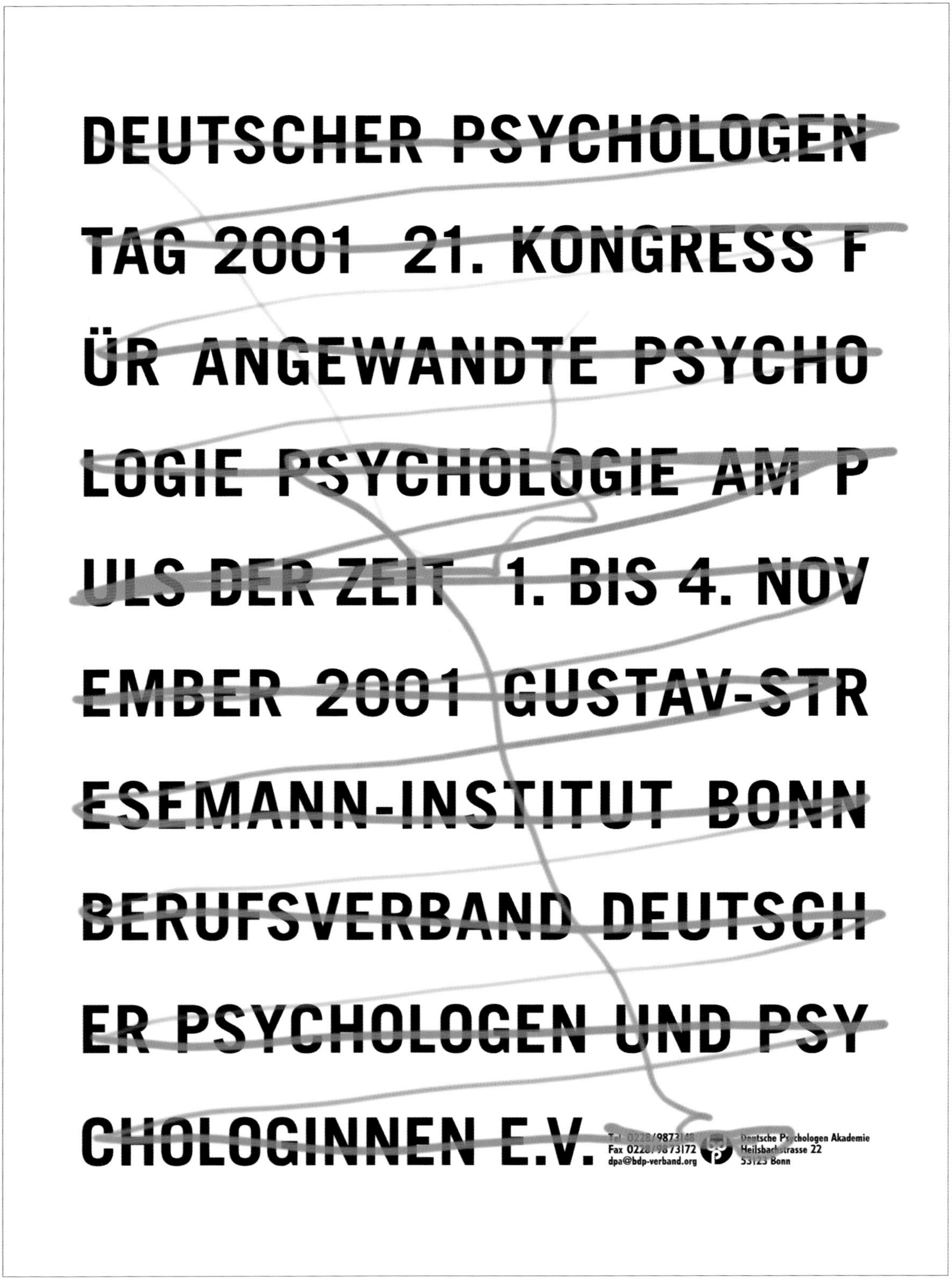

DEUTSCHER PSYCHOLOGEN
TAG 2001 21. KONGRESS F
ÜR ANGEWANDTE PSYCHO
LOGIE PSYCHOLOGIE AM P
ULS DER ZEIT 1. BIS 4. NOV
EMBER 2001 GUSTAV-STR
ESEMANN-INSTITUT BONN
BERUFSVERBAND DEUTSCH
ER PSYCHOLOGEN UND PSY
CHOLOGINNEN E.V.

Tel 0228/9873145
Fax 0228/9873172
dpa@bdp-verband.org

Deutsche Psychologen Akademie
Heilsbachstrasse 22
53123 Bonn

A poster and some conference gadgets. The red line traces the viewer's eye movement. The client ended up using the flashy greenyellowblue one. (67)

HI KARLSSONWILKER*

die sonne*, das licht*,
die stadt*, das geld*,
und der ruhm*, wie die blume im arbeitertum

kein zweifel, karlssonwilker*

die firma, cozy parties für ausländer* mit problemen*
die musik der welt im krieg mit dir zu hause
der sieg ist die freundin des helden im zweifel*

wieder karlssonwilker*

danach das glück*, immer immer wieder
die tränen der frauen*, das blut der feinde*,
...an seiner seite ein lächeln wie ihr schrei*

natürlich karlssonwilker*

wie feuer in illustrator*,...vegetarisches fummeln
schwitzende hanteln,...keine lust*,...zu teuer
der morgen danach*, atemlos der klient

immer karlssonwilker*

fettige haare*, alte jacke
kein geld, schlechte filme und billiges bier
...einsamkeit*, williamsburg trotzdem

klar karlssonwilker*

wie ein tier, mit dem kopf zwischen den schenkeln
yada yada...riding you that was fun
you are like the pellegrino* in my nose, never wasting time
just love*

maybe karlssonwilker*

your old school sneakers in my mouth,
your sweat saliva on my keyboard, your greasy doughnut
in my pants
you are the last glue trap,...hiding in a teddy bear from
sony music*

sooo karlssonwilker*

your wet photoshop* in my dreams, like a horny tongue
in my ear, breaking me down from within,...
while i'm eating your long hair on a 12' blimpie*

yup karlssonwilker*

rub me, rub me, it's a miracle*, it's a lie* at the last day of the
revolution, keeping me safe, like the dj* making me feel nice
in the century of you*

don't tell me why karlssonwilker*

Peter Stemmler, Creature Designer
Quickhoney

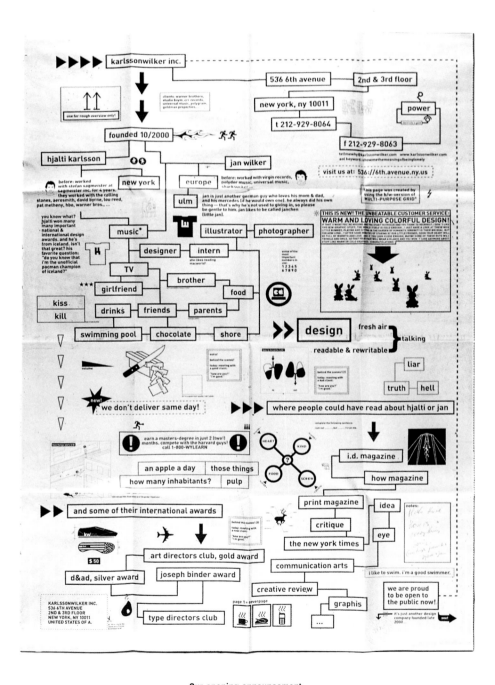

Our opening announcement.
It took us 2 months to design it and the printer completed his part in less than 2 hours. (69)

idea
eye
notes:
i like to swim. i'm a good swimmer.
we are proud to be open to the public now!
design

After 6 months in business we moved downstairs: more space, a fake fireplace, and the same price.
Bar, back room, and backyard rooftop included.

book I

How Things Work

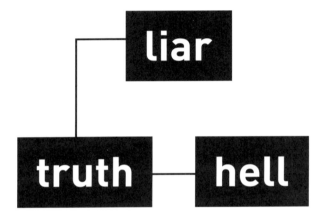

TINY STORIES (1):

my parents left me deep in the woods and told me not to follow
them. i did anyway and took up residence in the toolshed out
back. i snuck into the house during the day in order to eat and go
to the bathroom. at night i watched them through the windows.
sometimes when i am angry i kick over the garbage cans or steal
tools from the garage. they haven't suspected anything yet and i am
beginning to worry about their health. they don't eat right and they sit
too close to the tv.

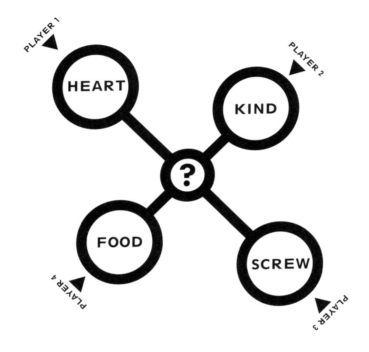

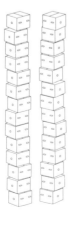

meeting with a good
client:

"how are you?"
"i'm good."

fresh air

} talking

readable & rewritable

i like to swim. i'm a good swimmer.

meeting with a bad
client:

"how are you?"
"i'm good."

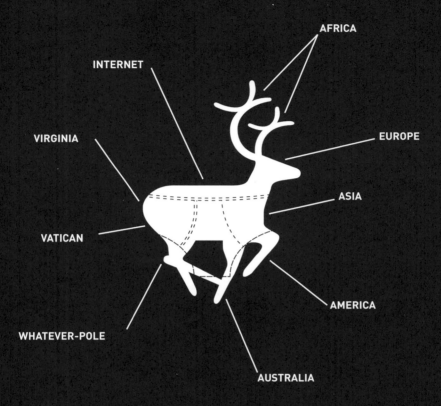

AFRICA

INTERNET

VIRGINIA

EUROPE

ASIA

VATICAN

AMERICA

WHATEVER-POLE

AUSTRALIA

TINY STORIES (2):
i wasn't there until about the middle and by that time everyone had already divided themselves into groups. i got stuck with some people who wouldn't even talk to me. i tried to complain about it but no one seemed to care. when i get some money together i am going to bust out of this place. until then i am going to keep my mouth shut and play nice. by the time they start suspecting that i am up to something i will already be well on my way to freedom.

f h

$ 50

complete the following sentence:

i am not ...., but ....! trust me.

use for rough overview only!

what a great proposal:
GREENPEACE

new! we don't deliver same day!

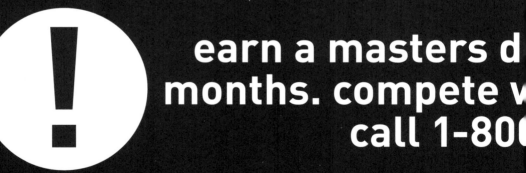

earn a masters d
months. compete v
call 1-80

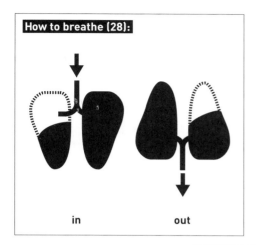

How to breathe (28):

in   out

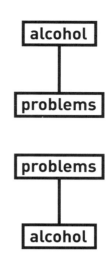

alcohol

problems

problems

alcohol

some of the
most
important
numbers in
use:

1 2 3 4 5
6 7 8 9 0

meeting with a new
client:

"how are you?"
"i'm good."

TINY STORIES (3):
my dad got into another drunk-driving accident the other day. i
saw him at the hospital and he still had a shard of metal sticking
out of his chest. he didn't have much to say, just asked me to
sneak him a beer. he also told me to mow the lawn. i was like,
what, that piece of shit hasn't been mowed in like three years. but,
well, i guess you should be nicer to sick people. i kept looking at
that shard, though. i was thinking, hey maybe i just pull this fucker
out. our eyes met and i figured it was time to go.

ee in just 2 (two!)
the harvard guys!
/HY LERN?

THIS IS NEW! THE UNBEATABL

WARM AND LOVING CO

IF THAT´S WHAT YOU´RE MISSING AND YOU START TO FREEZE
THIS B/W-GRAPHIC-STUFF, THE WORLD ITSELF IS COLD EN
LITTLE BUNNIES, PLAYING AND SITTING IN THE GARDEN OF H
FOR HOW LONG...? AFTER SOME MINUTES OF STARING AT OU
BE FULL OF WARMTH AND LOVE. AND IF YOU LOOK CLOSE E
TWINKLE AND SMILE, SO THAT YOUR FACE WILL WEAR A GLA
STUFF LIKE WARM OR COLD GRAPHICS. CONGRATULATIONS!

USTOMER SERVICE:

RFUL DESIGN!

OU THINK TO YOURSELF: I DON´T LIKE
..! JUST HAVE A LOOK AT THESE NICE
TY. VIRGINITY IS THEIR BIG GOAL, BUT
LE FRIENDS, SOON YOUR HEART WILL
, MAYBE SOME OF THESE GUYS WILL
D YOU WON´T CARE ANYMORE ABOUT

what to feed pigs: bread   things that other things land on: honey, butter, and maybe jelly   nice name for an elephant: pronto, the goalkeeper

insert coin →

kiss

kill

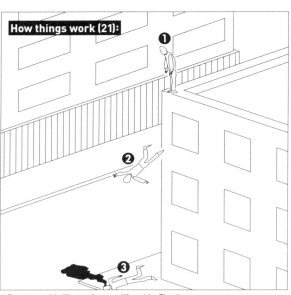

How things work (21):

❶

❷

❸

→ Do not use this illustration as a life guide. Thank you.

an apple a day

those things

how many inhabitants?

pulp

Am I normal?
Sometimes, I just have to draw this.

But check this out. Cool, eh?

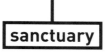

page 1 = coverpage

Congratulations to the winner of this year's "designers against violence" grand international poster competition:

because violence is bad!

notes:

THIS IS NEW! THE UNBEATABLE CUSTOMER SERVICE:

MARRYING OUTSIDE YOUR CASTE

THIS TOPIC ONLY MAKES SENSE AND APPLIES TO YOU IF YOU ARE IN A HIGHER CASTE THAN YOUR WANNABE PARTNER. SO: BREATHE IN, BREATHE OUT. COUNT TO TEN. IS IT REALLY WORTH IT? WHATEVER YOUR ANSWER IS, IT DOESN'T MATTER. YOU'LL GET DIVORCED ANYWAY. JUST MAKE SURE YOU'LL NOT GET KILLED FOR YOUR LIFE INSURANCE.

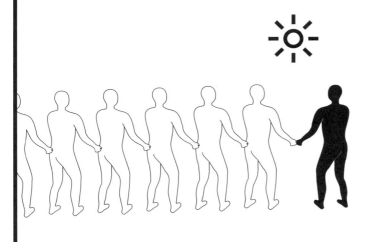

THIS IS NEW! THE UNBEATABLE CUSTOMER SERVICE:

BEING A SPECIALIST: NOW EVEN BETTER

YOU HAVE ANY SPECIAL SKILLS? GREAT! WE NEED YOU LIKE THIS. DON'T THINK FOR OTHER PEOPLE. THEY ARE ALL SPECIALLY TRAINED HUMANS, JUST LIKE YOU. PLUMBERS AS WELL AS PLUMBERS, ALL SPECIALISTS. BUT BEWARE: SOMETIMES PEOPLE HIDE BEHIND A CERTAIN SPECIALITY, JUST LIKE "I'M A POET." AND IF YOU'RE NOT SURE WHAT THEY REALLY ARE, JUST ASK THEM WHAT RHYMES WITH "STUPID" (THEY BETTER COME UP WITH AT LEAST FIVE WORDS, OR THEY'RE SCREWED!) NOW WE ALL CAN CONTINUE WITH OUR DUTY IN BEING SPECIALIZED GLOBAL CITIZENS.

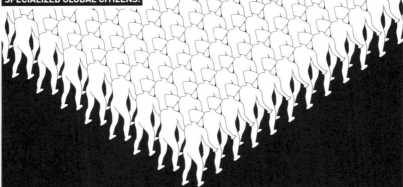

TINY STORIES (5):
i found a bird with a broken wing underneath my bedroom window. it had woken me up with it's chirping. i wrapped it in a small towel and fed it some bread crumbs. there aren't many trees around our house so i figured that the nest must be on our roof. my dad knocked on my door and i didn't have time to hide the bird. he wasn't angry, but he took it away from me. i never saw it again. when i was much older he told me that he had drowned it in the garage. ain't no hope for a bird with a broken wing, he said.

HANDWRITING
TERROR!
AhhhhL!
yeah!

the effect of drugs on designers:

the effect of drugs on breakfast:

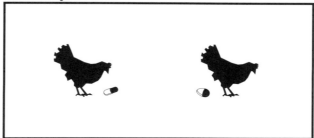

the effect of religion on male perception:

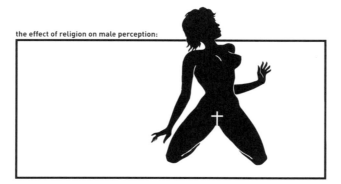

the effect of children on men:

hi! i'm a square inch! usually, i cannot speak.

volume

Story continued from page 26 **Again a friend phones with a recommendation. Stefan sends over Tony Goldman**, a New York–based real-estate developer and preservationist. He has played a large part in the revitalization of SoHo and now is planning to open a diner in an up-and-coming location in Philadelphia. Hjalti meets him in his office downtown and shows him the portfolio he put together for the Vitra meeting. Tony views it silently, considers it slowly, then says, "Great work." Hjalti is never certain that his presentation gets him the job; it is more likely Stefan's recommendation. But whatever it is, karlssonwilker is hired.

The restaurant is located near the University of Pennsylvania and is geared to a student market, serving burgers and beer. It gets its name from a set of letters that Gary Farmer, a long-time Goldman employee and the new restaurant's manager, found in a flea market. The seven letters offer just a few options—Red Line, Lie Nerd, El Diner—and the latter seems the obvious choice.

Gary plans to use his find for the restaurant's street signage, but the project entails a variety of other graphics: menus, coasters, a clock, matchbooks, tables, dishware, and more. Hjalti is very excited about this job. It is significant for the studio, an entire graphic package rather than a single piece.

Hjalti goes to Philadelphia to visit the diner, which is already under construction. Gary gives him a complete tour, from the soon-to-be entrance to the soon-to-be bathrooms. He is kind enough to Hjalti, but the New Yorker senses he is a bit put off by having been excluded from choosing his restaurant's graphic designers. Hjalti is unfettered and goes about his work. He photographs El Diner's found letters and starts the job by setting them as white text in a blue-green box.

Jan returns to New York for a nine-day visit. Nine days is just enough time to put together the proposal with Hjalti and to find an apartment of his own. He gets a sublet on Avenue B, a large and beautiful one-bedroom, and splits it with a friend from Stuttgart. Hjalti's apartment is now free, but Hjalti is too happy living with Vera to return there. He enjoys his daily walk from the West Village to Fourteenth Street and back again. His excitement for the Upper West Side has waned.

After a long six weeks away from New York, Jan is ready to dive into work. He likes what Hjalti has done with the found letters for El Diner and suggests using them as a base for an entire alphabet. That way, the type style can be used for more than just the restaurant's name, but for all the copy in the project. For Hjalti and Jan do not want to plaster "El Diner" all over the place—that would be too easy and boring. They draw a font called, appropriately enough, "El Font." This simple type coupled with a blue-green color becomes the basis for all the design work to come.

The designers approach the job as "a diner with an attitude," a diner that talks to its customers. This means coming up with engaging texts for its many design elements. They write chatty copy above the bar: a list of all the countries in the world, as well as facts about Columbus, Elvis, and Brazil. Then they write copy for its toothpicks ("this is what happens to naughty little trees," "dentists make on average $120,000 a year"), sugar packets ("long pillow for tiny people,"

65

"captured hourglass fugitives"), plates, business cards, and pencils. They write this copy for a New York real-estate developer, but they also write it for themselves. Their playful T-shirt texts include "twentyfour ours" and "polish my cock ring"—aphorisms not usually targeted to restaurateurs.

Hjalti and Jan know their client will either hate this proposal or love it. It does not allow for any middle ground. They present their work just days before Christmas at Goldman Properties. Hjalti warns Jan that the SoHo office is a bit intimidating, as it is built around Tony's oversized desk. So for this meeting the pair trade in their jeans and T-shirts for suits. They present fifty-four boards of design work, showing everything they can think of. After the third board, Tony starts laughing, and his employees know it is safe to join in with him. Tony is so excited that he calls Gary during the meeting and describes the work over the phone, bringing him in on the fun.

The partners have never been so happy to get a job. Their presentation is a big success. They insist that this has little to do with how popular "polish my cock ring" is with Tony's employees. In fact, they hate to be called out as "funny" designers. They insist that their office is built upon their good design sense, not their good sense of humor, which is true. Still, some of their work, especially the copy for El Diner and their self-promotional design, is hilarious.

The designers return to their office, giddy with their success, to find that all their hard work has disappeared. Their brand new G4—the computer dedicated to El Diner—has died, taking all their files with it. The good news is that it is the only job on the computer and it can be retrieved without too much trouble. The bad news is that their repairman charges by the size of the hard drive, not the amount of data, so karlssonwilker is out $1000 and a few days of anxious worrying.

Christmas brings another break to the work on El Diner. Jan flies back to Germany, where he remains until mid-January. Hjalti spends Christmas with Vera in Iceland, and stays on for two weeks. The restaurant is slated to open in February, so when they return to the office, Hjalti and Jan work frantically on the job, filling their evenings and weekends. They produce a wall clock for the restaurant right in their office. For all the other pieces, they draw up specific details and send these off to manufacturers that Tony has used on previous projects. The studio is happy to see how many of its designs are actually executed. Even the word magnets they propose for customers to create their own copy on the bathroom walls are made—although the "polish my cock ring" T-shirts are not.

The money from this job carries karlssonwilker for a few months. The restaurant, sadly, lasts only a little longer than that. In fact, Hjalti and Jan never get to see their finished work, not even the magnets, which, they learn, students have been flushing down the toilets. For some reason the University of Pennsylvania, who owns the lease to El Diner, shuts it down and does not allow its owners to rescue the design pieces left behind.

It is a new year, a time for new clients. The partners, however, do not know how to go about finding fresh ones. Hjalti has been living in New York for eight years, but all of his business contacts are other designers. Jan does not know anybody. And the pair's idea of interacting with the New York design community is meeting people at AIGA events; they go, but they often end up standing in the corner by themselves.

Although karlssonwilker's build-it-and-they-will-come business plan might seem somewhat naive, it also seems wonderfully optimistic. The partners have reason for their confidence. Hjalti came to New York on his $13,000 lottery win; surely he has good luck on his side. Jan is hopeful by nature; who else would start a surfing apparel company in the middle of Germany? Both men had been raised in comfortable families, which brings them a certain expectation for success and the security of help in case of failure. This help comes in handy now. Work has been steady, if slow, but pay for that work can take up to three months. Hjalti watches as the money flows out of the office. Landlords and utilities and all the other business expenses cannot wait, and so the office account is running down. Though the thirty-three-year-old feels awful about it, he picks up the phone and calls his parents again for help.

Jan does the same, and his father comes through with both a check and a job. Dr. Wilker is the director of the academy of the German Psychology Union, and he asks his son to design an identity package for their upcoming conference. This includes a poster, T-shirts, a bag, and a binder—all the typical conference stuff. Karlssonwilker proposes adding a candy "pill bottle" to the list. Jan already did work for the academy a couple years earlier, work that they did not use. Dr. Wilker convinces him to try again, noting that Jan needs to learn to win over clients, and he accepts (easing, no doubt, the feeling of guilt that comes with his father's loan).

Karlssonwilker's proposal is straightforward black copy with an overlay of red lines, tracing the route the eye takes in reading the copy. (Jan learned some lessons like this from participating in his father's research as a child.) Hjalti and Jan are fond of this design, but their clients are not. For them the work belongs in a museum, not at a conference. They send it back with a request to try again. Hjalti and Jan refuse. Sure, the money would help them out, but they are afraid that trying again will likely be pointless, as their vision does not seem to mesh with the academy's. Concurrently, Jan's father visits New York, and the dutiful son and recipient of emergency gifts of his father's cash sits down and becomes Dr. Wilker's designer for the day, creating a poster to better fit the clients' sense of style. Dr. Wilker returns to Germany with a design centered on a brightly colored cell phone, and the academy sends karlssonwilker a welcome check.

Through it all, Hjalti and Jan are loving their space. They have made it their own with their furniture, some potted plants, and a singing Backstreet Boys poster, and are happy to spend most of their time—days, evenings, weekends—in it designing and chatting and hanging out. It is more than their office: it is their fort. They eat most of their meals there, donuts in the morning, Chinese food in the afternoon, fast food in the evening. The delivery guys know without asking to add two Cokes to their orders. Their girlfriends join them there in the evenings, and they open up their hangout to other friends as well. One guy recovers from a lost job and a lost girlfriend by spending his nights hacking away on karlssonwilker's computers. He marks himself as the office sidekick by pasting his picture in the back window of a remote-controlled car they keep in their office. He adds Jan in the driver seat and Hjalti riding shotgun.

Hjalti and Jan also love their new office for its party potential. They both like parties and throw them every couple of months—for Hjalti's August birthday, for the Halloween parade that crosses under their window, or for no reason at all. At one bash, Hjalti's cousin makes off with a plastic Jesus nightlight they have bought especially for the space, but most events are pretty tame, if drunken. The office's typically empty mini-refrigerator is filled with Budweisers on party nights. Hjalti and Jan like to time their soirées to when the office needs a good cleaning. They do a little pick-up before their guests arrive, then spend the day after—a hungover family day—with Hjalti and Vera and Jan and Ella cleaning up the mess of the party along with the general office mess.

These are not the first get-togethers in the space. A previous tenant had rented it out for private events, and now and then people come over asking for, you know, the parties. It had also once been a brothel, and every once in a while some biker guys stop by asking for, you know, the girls. But Hjalti and Jan have no girls to offer. This is a disappointment to their super, Mr. Sal, who asks if they can hook him up with "some of those nice women" he sees going in and out of their office.

Really Really Getting Started.
These are happy days for karlssonwilker. So why is Jan in agony? His back is killing him. He cannot figure out why; his days moving furniture and doing the limbo are history now. But he is in such bad shape that he visits an emergency room, where a doctor examines him and gives him a prescription for a muscle relaxant. Karlssonwilker has no health insurance program, so Jan is due for more pain from the hospital bill. A kind woman at the admissions desk suggests he enter the wrong address on his form, and so he is saved from that, at least.

One cause of Jan's pain may be stress making its way into the office. When the job for Jan's father is finished, the only design to occupy karlssonwilker is what the partners create for them-selves. And while money is not pouring in, it is flowing out. Hjalti shares Jan's pain. Hardware, soft-ware, office supplies, and donuts all add up, and now Hjalti is having nightmares about the Verizon bill. For this kind of pain, they need more than muscle relaxants.

If the clients are not coming to them, they must go to the clients. Their girlfriends have encouraged them since they opened their business to be active in pursuing new work. For months, their suggestions have fallen on deaf ears, but now Hjalti and Jan realize they are right. They pick up the phones and dial some ad agencies and record companies to ask for interviews. After a few painful cold calls, they give this up. It is just not cool to beg for business. There is a lot they will do to keep their studio alive, but they see begging as a clear sign of an early failure. When the guy at the other end of the phone asks, "So, you guys are slow, huh?" it makes them feel that much worse. They go back to busying themselves with their personal design.

Having no paid work allows them to spend time thinking about how to present themselves. So, five months into their partnership, karlssonwilker announces the opening of its office. This is what real companies do, right? And this is what Vera and Ella have been pushing their boyfriends to do since they started the business. Hjalti and Jan decide to produce a color poster and mail it out. (They do not recognize the humor in this choice so soon after Jan's renunciation of the medium.) People will open it, like it, and say, "I must hire them!" The few projects of their first few months do not quite fill up a poster, however, so they add video stills of their photogenic office to fill in space. But the poster still feels empty. They include some work they did with Stefan, despite some reservations. When they show this to him, he politely tells them it is weird to see his studio's work under their name. Hjalti and Jan recognize this is true, yet worry about filling the open spaces when they take it out.

At this point, after many hours of working on the design, they bid out the job to see how much the poster will cost. The $2,500 fee is far more than they should spend, so they move to plan B—a two-page black-and-white mailer on newsprint. Karlssonwilker is an office on a budget. Announcing themselves as one is not necessarily a bad thing. And newsprint suggests a design direction. They fill the outer page of the mailer with line illustrations, all drawn on the computer. A few are reused from Jan's design for *No Eats Yes*, but most are new works. These include two people carrying a box, portraits of Hjalti and Jan, and a trio of steaming coffee, chicken, and cell phone. The designers put their ideas into several flow charts scattered about the page. Each is comprised of boxed texts, which Jan used on *No Eats Yes*. Some give basic, useful, business data, like contact information and a list of clients. Some are just fun; one chart links "liar," "truth," and "hell" (similar to the chart on the back of this book linking "rich," "beautiful," and "poor"). Nothing really flows in the charts, but they give the impression that something very logical is happening at karlssonwilker.

The mailer's centerfold shows a full-page photograph of Hjalti and Jan. They mock up an idea by scanning a random suit from a magazine and Photoshopping it under their heads, stretching it a bit under Jan to reach his height. Then they buy matching suits and have a friend photograph them all dressed up. Somehow, the shots just do not work as well as the rough mock-up so they go back to that and add a few chalk lines, outlining how a tailor might correct the cuffs, sleeves, and lapels of the suits to correct their fit. Hjalti wears an outline of a pencil at his breast pocket, while Jan dons a heart at his. When questioned now about using their young attractive selves to sell their design services, they claim they only included their portraits to fill up space, since they did not have much work to show. But they are forced to admit that all of the jobs that came as a result of the mailer came from women.

69

They take the finished piece to a local printer who specializes in religious and political pamphlets. After weeks of working on the design, Hjalti and Jan are surprised that the printing itself takes less than two hours. They carry their bundles—still warm from the press—back to the office, where they fold them up, place them in simple gray envelopes, and rubber stamp them with, "We are proud to be open to the public now! Brand new! A new design company is born! A fresh formation is on the run! Blabla!"

At the beginning of the project, they choose special postage stamps to use on the mailers, printed in beautiful black-and-white to match their design. They even choose the font for the address labels to match the typeface of the stamp. But by the time they finish designing and printing their announcement, the stamps are no longer available at their local post office. They go to New York's main post office in midtown, and they too are out. They finally find what they designed for at a philatelic center, and procure enough to cover the three hundred contacts on the mailing list they buy.

Finally, the mailers go out, each with a personal, hand-written message in a box left empty for "notes." They write personalized remarks to their friends ("Hey, Constantin. Hope all is well. All our best to Laurene.") as well as people they do not know ("Hello, John. How is Alabama?"). After fifty signatures, their comments change to "I've written 50 in a row, I can't write any more"; after one hundred they write, "If you can read this, call us." Hjalti and Jan get a lot of kind responses from friends, and a couple of unexpected ones from people like Michael Bierut of Pentagram. They even get a few jobs from this.

But first they get another job from Vera. Hjalti's girlfriend has moved on from Landor to work as the art director at Anne Klein. She is there only a short time when she invites Hjalti and Jan to do some work for her. Jan goes on this interview alone and meets with Vera and Dee Solomon, Anne Klein's senior vice president of marketing. He has already met Dee socially, but is nervous about this professional encounter. He is still somewhat frustrated with his English, and Vera has suggested that he will have to sell himself a bit to get this job. He compensates for both concerns by trying too hard. When Dee presents the project, an update of Anne Klein's lion logo, Jan enthusiastically responds that he has done just this kind of work for a firm in Munich. Dee asks him who the company is, and Jan says he forgets. It is a true story—he really did this work—but his nerves have made his mind blank. He remembers the nickname he gave his Munich client, but it is not something to repeat in polite company. Fortunately, Dee is forgiving. Jan continues to struggle through the interview, and she continues to be kind.

Jan leaves Anne Klein with the lion file, and he works on it back at his office, creating several new variations of the logo. When he brings them back, Dee is not pleased with any of the solutions. But Jan claims that this is his intention. By getting reactions to each version he can find out what kind of lion is appropriate—a smiling lion, a sincere lion. He takes her responses back again, and finishes the job in two days. Dee and Vera are happy with his work, and Hjalti is saved from the strangeness of working for his girlfriend again.

Tony Goldman calls Hjalti and Jan. The bad news is that El Diner is el finito. The good news is that he has a new project for them. This time it is a restaurant closer to home, a tavern in downtown New York. Stone Street Tavern will not suffer from the downscale market of El Diner's student clientele. Instead, it will cater to the local Wall Street crowd. Tony wants a traditional tavern with a twist, so he wants Hjalti and Jan.

This project comes without found letters, so the designers choose some classic fonts from their small font library. The twist comes in their application. On its main entrance facing Stone Street, the signage is straightforward, while on its rear facade on Pearl Street it is written backwards. (The poor guy charged with painting the sign has to put up with all the passersby telling him he is doing his job wrong.) Hjalti and Jan design a faux-historic marker for this side, reading, "Dearest Customer. You are in front of the back of our lovely tavern. Just walk around the corner and you will find yourself in front of the historic Stone Street Tavern. Welcome."

Along with their ideas for the look of the tavern, the partners propose a slogan for it: "The House of the Moving Stone." Hjalti and Jan do more than design some signs and mugs, they create an entire mythology for this brand new tavern on a very old street. According to their story, there is a two-million-pound rock 250,000 feet in diameter under the basement of the building, though the patrons of Stone Street Tavern will be able to see only the tip of it poking through the floor in the corner. This rock moves like a pendulum at a snail's pace. They even have a diagram to prove it.

Tony likes the graphics Hjalti and Jan show him, but he kills the moving-stone idea. Instead, he goes with another of their proposals: "Since 1656." That this applies to Stone Street rather than Stone Street Tavern matters little. It works. The designers set this and other traditionalist lines— "proudly taking care of thirst and hunger," "serving the public since the early century," "the finest quality in food and goods"—in their traditionalist type on the off-white background of matches, coasters, business cards, caps, and T-shirts. Soon enough the pair celebrate a job well done and a nice fat check with dinner at the tavern, eating off their designed plates and drinking out of their designed mugs.

Jan and Hjalti are typically happy to celebrate closer to home. The bodega at Fourteenth and Sixth is as good a spot as any. The bartender—otherwise known as the Korean proprietor—already knows Jan by name ("Mr. Germany"). There is a warm and lovely room—the flower department—where they can hang out. There are interesting people—customers and the guy who cuts the flowers—to chat with. And the beer is cheap. One night they share over a dozen beers there. It is a very good night. Still Hjalti is a bit embarrassed by it all, and afterward does not visit the bodega for a few days.

In March 2001, Hjalti and Jan spend more time working on their "identity." They design business cards, expecting that they will need a lot of them for all the interviews that are bound to come pouring in from the mailers. These follow the look of the mailer: simple copy in a simple black box, which becomes their logo by default. Jan knows a guy in Germany who can silkscreen the cards inexpensively. He prints samples using white on black and black on vellum. Hjalti and Jan decide on a black-and-white-on-white design and print four sets, one for Hjalti Karlsson, one for Jan Wilker, one for "the intern," and one blank—all for $600. But even this small bill is too much for karlssonwilker. Jan hides his head from his printer friend for five months until he can scratch up the money, then mails it along with a $50 forgive-me fee.

This is not the studio's first attempt to design business cards for themselves. The partners worked on an alternate design when they were first setting up their office. They set their name and address in bold red type, printed the text on adhesive sheets, cut it out, and attached it to business cards that they had collected from Landor, Interbrand, Pentagram, and the like. It is a distinctive approach, but they decide that this type of appropriation is better suited for an activist practice than for their own office. And so they use it instead for the loosely knit group that calls itself Parasite Design, which Hjalti and Jan started with a few of their friends. The group is frustrated with the impossible costs of hardware and software, the inflexible policies of most tech companies, and the unfair advantage of large design and advertising firms that use their pricey office tools for a maximum of ten hours a day, leaving them silent for the other fourteen. Parasite Design regularly breaks into such offices at night, using key counterfeits and other tricks, dodging the occasional security guard or cleaning person. Once inside, they help themselves to the free tools and power supply, gorging themselves on the excess. They cannot give away too much more here, but let us just say that Parasite Design continues to thrive today. So far, none of its founding members has spent a night in jail.

But back to karlssonwilker. One more item will round out their identity—logo T-shirts and sweatshirts to send to their friends and clients. They design four motifs: "karlssonwilker" on an Uzi, "karlssonwilker" on a loaf of bread being sliced, black goo being spread onto "karlssonwilker" T-shirt-shaped bread, and "karlssonwilker" on a remote control (no doubt inspired by the one they use to control their little red car). Jan has Sharksucker, his former surfing apparel company, print the shirts. They also make some embroidery labels with karlssonwilker's new logo. Hjalti and Jan plan to attach these to bathrobes for really important clients, but so far have only stuck them on their portfolios.

Worries.

It is March 2001. Almost three months have passed since Jan and Ella returned to the U.S. They still have no visas, and so will have to return to Germany and wait it out for a while. Jan cannot face another few months away from his studio and so considers an alternate plan. He has heard that if he can get his passport stamped he can state that he has been away from the States and thus extend his stay. Canada is the closest border crossing, so he and Ella pack up and take the drive north. They make a little vacation out of their effort, spending one lovely day at Niagara Falls and another in Toronto. Then they head for home.

At the border they proudly hold out their passports for review and are waved on through. No stop, no search, and no stamps. This is not the plan. They chat by the side of the road and decide to try another crossing. But the next is the same—no stamp. Jan is desperate. He has spent his limited funds renting the car for this trip and he has nothing to show for it. He cannot go back to Germany without a fight. He turns to the border patrolman and coyly asks him, "Well, what about my stamp?" The patrolman points him in the direction of the customs office. It seems Jan and Ella are not the only people who have heard about the Canadian-stamp trick. The customs officer is ready for them. He asks if they know that what they are attempting is illegal. Jan feigns innocence, but soon enough gives it up. He pleads that he is a student who loves America and cannot bear to leave it. His songs of praise fall on deaf ears. He and Ella go back to New York, and on to Germany, and then Jan comes back alone.

By April the question marks in karlssonwilker's spreadsheets have become real numbers, and their $30,000 start-up fund, based on what Hjalti and Jan (and their parents) had rather than what they needed, is quickly dwindling. It is an unusual time to expand the office, but fate calls. Their landlord catches the tenants downstairs from karlssonwilker living in their office space and nails a letter to the door telling them to move out. From this letter, which he cannot help but read, Hjalti finds out that the second-floor space is $100 per month less expensive than theirs. And one night, when he finds its door cracked open, he discovers that it is even nicer. It is larger, lighter, and has an outdoor roof deck and a built-in wet bar. He and Jan dream of adding this to their current office, maybe filling it with lots of employees or using it as a gallery to show friends' work. But they know that the extra $1,100 a month is really not feasible for them and so let their friends know that their old office is now available to sublet. Another graphic designer, Paul Sahre, is happy to take up their offer. He brings along his little dog, Sid, who quickly becomes 536 Sixth Avenue's mascot and official greeter. But for a month and a half, Hjalti and Jan have two full floors to themselves. To this day, their business cards read "2nd and 3rd floor."

New neighbors move to the fourth floor at the same time. They are a postcard printing company—or are they? They have a lot of strange visitors, people who seem to be looking for something other than postcards and leave plastic bags of weed by the entrance. They talk to Hjalti and Jan about installing a video camera, an iron gate, and a window in the front door. Two weeks after they move in, they claim their safe has been looted by an "insider." Paul is instantly nervous about these neighbors and is ready to abandon his new office. But by early November, they leave the building. There is no more need for the iron gate.

April is also the time for a new intern, Jan's cousin Miriam Wilker. She has not seen Jan in about ten years, but now that he co-owns a New York design firm she gives him a call and arranges to come to work. She arrives at the same time as a new project for CRI, guitarist and composer Scott Fields' *96 Gestures*. Miriam and Jan design blue lines on the case to cover parts of the black text on the liner. Though there may be similarities between this and Jan's work for the German Psychology Union—indicating some kind of familial connection between himself, his father, and his cousin—Jan denies any imitation. Things continue to go well with CRI. Bryan Conley, their production manager, is a fan of karlssonwilker and gives them free range with their designs. This makes working for the small fee worthwhile. The designers relish the pure fun and integrity of the job.

While they work on *96 Gestures*, Hjalti and Jan design a postcard for CRI's participation in the JVC Jazz Festival. It is an ugly postcard, and it is officially credited to the Brooklyn design studio that oversaw its production, so let us just forget it.

CRI brings another project to the office the next month. Hjalti works on the first version, Jan and Miriam on the second, and Hjalti on the final presentation. This one is called *No Images*, so the first thing the designers discuss is the image to go on its cover. They choose "big sky," a stock image sample that comes with every Photoshop package, to print in black and white on the liner, then silkscreen yellow on the clear case. This is the first time they use this technique in the Blueshift series. They like silkscreening for its wide range of color options, but in the end, they decide that hot-stamping produces a stronger, more solid effect.

It is not all work work work, mixed in with a bit of worry, at karlssonwilker. Once in a while the two friends shut down their computers and play with their other office toys. There is the remote-controlled car already mentioned, with Jan still in the driver's seat. There are little balls and clips and scraps and who-knows-what that Hjalti methodically tosses in the air or back and forth between his hands. And there is the office's favorite toy, a big black PlayStation that takes up the entire center of their fireplace. Even when the designers are bleary-eyed from a day in front of the computer screen, they can still see well enough to spend an hour or two with their joy sticks. Hjalti is a natural; he once scored higher than Iceland's reigning Pac Man champion. Jan holds his own.

And then it is back to work. Jan brings a CD job to the office. This is a nice change for him. He has relied on Hjalti's New York contacts for close to a year now and is ready to use his German connections. This comes from his comrade Hellmut Hattler, for whom Jan designed two CDs—*Sonic Tools* and *No Eats Yes*—before teaming up with Hjalti. Hellmut and his 1960s jazz fusion group Kraan

from the free alcohol. Their lamp is auctioned for $350, a good amount for the evening. In the months to come, WSF often features their design in its publicity material, as does karlssonwilker. People even call up to order a doggy of their own, but without connections to the Italian dog model manufacturer, there will be no more canine lamps.

Worries would not be complete without a new job from dad. In June it comes from Hjalti's father, a retired bank manager who now does consulting work for a small real-estate company. He had asked his son to design a logo for it a year ago, and finally Hjalti's guilt—and desperation—is enough to get him to work. He spends an hour on it, makes an ink stamp of his design, and mails it off to Iceland. He is so embarrassed by it that he claims Jan designed it. Hjalti's father sends a sample of how bad it looks on a piece of paper, the letters so fat they run into each other, and signs it, "Great logo. Say hello to Jan." No one is too happy, but no one is too upset. The work Hjalti's and Jan's fathers commission from them makes it a bit easier for them to hand over some money to their sons, and a bit easier for the struggling designers to accept it.

July 2001 starts off on a high note. Karlssonwilker receives word from *Novum*, a German graphic design magazine, that it will be featured in their January issue. Hjalti and Jan had sent their mailer to three German magazines and through this find their first bit of publicity. This good news is offset by problems with Jan's housing situation. He lost his sublet on Avenue B upon his return from Germany, and Vera found him a new place on Suffolk Street, slightly smaller and slightly cheaper. Now he is kicked out of this short-lived home. He has been paying for his sublet faithfully, but the leaseholders have used his money some other way, and the landlord has not received their rent for many months. It is a typical New York story, but here a personal one.

More bad news arrives with karlssonwilker's last job for CRI, a pair of CDs called *Quartet Lucy* and *Claudia Quintet* for drummer and composer John Hollenbeck. Brian Conley, Hjalti and Jan's supporter at CRI, has left the company. Their work is now handled by an outside firm that has produced other CRI design projects. Things start out well between them and karlssonwilker. The firm sends the designers a fan email, letting them know how much it likes their work. But fans can turn on you. When Hjalti and Jan submit their designs, the production crew claims they have prepared them incorrectly. It is unclear how this submission is different than any previous CRI submissions, but the firm claims that they have caused a production problem. More likely, the absence of Brian has caused the problem. The former fans think Hjalti and Jan are too much trouble and should not get any more work from Blueshift. This becomes a moot point when the label folds, but it still leaves a sour taste in Hjalti's and Jan's mouths. For Jan this is a fine way to end things. He thinks the *Claudia Quintet* is the best design of the series. It is Hjalti's least favorite.

Karlssonwilker's next intern follows a curiously similar love/hate path. When he first arrives he seems happy enough to work with Hjalti and Jan, but soon quits, walking out in the middle of the day. His excuses about competing school work are not very convincing, and the partners begin to wonder what it is about them that is turning people away.

Hjalti and Jan need some help getting their act back together, and their client Dee Solomon offers it. She puts them in touch with Rick Albert, a friend and a former ad agency owner. Rick is a man in his late forties, a guy who commands respect and charges a consulting fee to match. He appears to be connected to everybody, and karlssonwilker hopes he can bring them some interesting work. Instead he lectures them on the importance of the business end of their studio. It is the same thing their girlfriends have been telling them for months.

Rick is right. They do need to focus on their business. Jan and Hjalti had expected that design would be their office's biggest challenge. But instead it has turned out to be the easiest part of running an office. Design does not always come quickly to them, but it always does come, if after hours of work. Money is not that certain an equation; a lot of work does not mean an eventual windfall. If they kept time sheets they would be horrified to see their hourly rate.

Money troubles do not make it into Jan's thesis project on setting up a design office in New York. Instead, he puts together a PDF slide show of all the office's successes, which means most of its designs. He flies off to Stuttgart in July to present it and returns with his master's diploma, his work visa, and his girlfriend. They are happy to have an office to come back to. Without an apartment, or the money to pay for one, they must make it their new home. This prospect is a little scary, as the previous tenants had been thrown out of the space for living in it. They are going to have to be very careful, dodging the super, Mr. Sal, who they still have not set up with "some of those nice women," and the store owner who always seems to be hovering downstairs. Karlssonwilker has a new intern, Jean Lee, one of Paul Sahre's students. Her presence also makes their secret life more difficult. Jean is surprised to see Jan at work when she arrives every morning, and jokes that Jan is there so often he seems to live there. Jan laughs this off.

Jan keeps the lights off in case someone who would care happens by. Luckily the summer days offer long hours of sunlight. He and Ella pay $75 a month to join a nearby gym so they can take showers. Jan borrows an air mattress from a friend and sets it up each night in the front room of the office, a little island between the wet bar and the work area; each morning he crams it into a closet in the back room, next to his and Hjalti's twice-worn suits.

Jan and Ella soon acquire other roommates. The first is Matthias Ernstberger, a friend whom Jan knows from school. He is in town interviewing for a job with Stefan. He takes the sofa in the back room, making himself at home on its threadbare upholstery and broken springs. He is completely comfortable in this hostel, a little too comfortable for Hjalti, who is not used to walking into his office and seeing a bare-chested man brushing his teeth while Web surfing on his computer. But this roommate is nothing compared to karlssonwilker's uninvited guests. Mice have lodged themselves inside the roof of the office/bedroom and like to scamper around, their little feet tap-dancing on the tin ceiling at all hours. Karlssonwilker complains to their landlord, and he sends over an exterminator with glue traps and some more serious stuff. The critters soon go, except for "Frank," the mouse Paul Sahre keeps as a pet.

Blowing Jobs.

Karlssonwilker is twenty for twenty. They have completed every job they have taken on—an accomplishment for any firm. They have not always left their clients with smiles on their faces and promises of more work, but they have always finished what they have started and been paid in full. Sooner or later, their luck might change, and it changes now.

The first job that they blow is for Pandisc Records, a small Miami-based label. Beth Sereni, its A+R manager, likes their mailer and gives them a call about a new CD for Miami-based DJ Baby Anne, *Dark Side of the Boom*. Anne already has a particular photographer in mind to shoot the job, a New Yorker with whom she has worked on previous releases. Hjalti and Jan are not overly impressed with these covers—they seem rather conservative for a woman making headway in new music—so they prepare detailed directions for the shoot. For thirty minutes they painstakingly review their design with the photographer, explaining the extreme horizontal shots they need to wrap the entire CD case. He listens, nods, and takes their sketches with him to Miami. He comes back with a typical portrait in front of a typical ocean, cropped in a typical way. It has nothing to do with their art direction and cannot possibly be used to wrap around the case. They call Beth in desperation, explaining their problem and asking for a reshoot. Pandisc does not have the time or budget for this, and Hjalti and Jan cannot work with the photos, so the job ends in a stalemate. Another designer uses the typical shot, adding some typical type to give it an altogether typical look.

Hjalti and Jan are crushed. *Dark Side of the Boom* seemed to have so much potential—a client who appreciates their work, an up-and-coming young artist, and a small and presumably experimental label. All of this somehow adds up to a failed job. The failure also means they will get only a third of their fee, and, they presume, no more work from Beth.

It is one of those steamy August-in-New-York days. Hjalti arrives at the studio at ten, as usual, careful not to enter until Jan's air mattress is safely stowed away. He carries a glazed donut for himself and coffee and a French cruller for Jan. He checks out the morning's email, some greetings from Iceland and Germany, while Jan lights up a cigarette and plays a bit on the computer, waiting for the morning to pass until the time when he and his partner are at their working best.

Their reverie is broken by a ringing phone. It is Mary Fagot from Virgin Records. She, too, has seen their mailer and wants them to work on a CD, poster, and TV trailer for a new band called Moth. She sends over the music, and Jan and Hjalti start right in. They are inspired less by the band's songs than by its titles. The name of its slated first single, "I See Sound" suggests to them a guy with a camera mounted on a backpack, which he uses to view the space he steps into. This scheme would work well for both the CD and the single's video. Mary is won over by the proposal, but Moth's front man, Brad Stenz, is not so easy. So the designers try again with explorations of images (a leaping cheetah with some grazing cows) and type (over a dozen symbols of how "moth" could look). In one proposal they use three-dimensional type, flying off in different directions, to reflect the complexity of the name of the CD, *Provisions, Fiction, and Gear*.

Brad is still not happy. He claims that when he was writing the songs for the CD, he was thinking of some lonesome guy in a hotel room. Now he wants that vision on the cover. Hjalti and Jan do not know how to respond. They have been hired as the project's art directors and expect to be able to direct things. But the roles in designing CDs are not always so clear cut. Musicians are creative people and often feel that their conception for their album should include its packaging. Often, their idea includes some outdated view of what an album should look like—the alone-in-a-hotel-room thing has been done to death by this point. Sometimes they win this argument, sometimes the label wins, and sometimes the designer wins. In this case, the hotel room wins, so Hjalti and Jan make the best of it, shelving their camera backpack idea for a later date.

Hjalti flies out to LA to art-direct the photo shoot. If he must use a hotel room, at least he can use it his way. He encourages the photographer away from the cliché shots of empty hallways and single beds to focus in on pieces of the room. He takes these images back to New York, and the studio makes them even more abstract, cropping them to only the textured red of wallpaper, the yellow padding of a vinyl couch, the plush of a blue rug. At the same time, they work on the TV trailer. In it the words "Moth" and "I See Sound" flicker as black dots onto a complex yellow background, making themselves wholly apparent for only a microsecond before the screen is covered with dots. Moth is not crazy about either treatment. Brad and his band lose interest in karlssonwilker, and vice versa. Hjalti and Jan's streak of twenty completed projects is now followed by two blown projects. Worst of all, they will never hear from Virgin again, a client they would love to keep.

But both Mary Fagot and Beth Sereni will return to karlssonwilker with more jobs. They apparently came away from *Provisions, Fiction, and Gear* and *Dark Side of the Boom* with good feelings for the designers and their work. Hjalti and Jan have a hard time sensing this. They are not able to accept that the way they present themselves is not unprofessional and that their insistence on good design does not go unappreciated. Instead, they refuse to stop believing that one bad experience means a failed relationship. Story continues on page 129

80

To: Michelle Yung and Hannes Schleinkofer
Regarding: details 4/01
Today is: 04 / 19 / 01
Yesterday was: 04 / 18 / 01
Total Page count: 4

Hi there, Michelle and hello Hannes,

please see attached sheets for details.
talk to you soon.

jan

From:

karlssonwilker inc.
536 6th avenue
2nd & 3rd floor
new york city 10011
212 929 8064
fax 929 8063
www.karlssonwilker.inc

This is a LETTER.

Hello there Lili.

We have been the biggest fans of elektra for years...
Yes, we would love and kill to get this idea through.

Just give us a ring and everything will be fine.

Hope you are good.

All the best from 6th ave.

Jan & Hjalti

karlssonwilker inc.
536 6th avenue
2nd & 3rd floor
new york city 10011
212 929 8064
fax 929 8063
www.karlssonwilker.com

This is an INVOICE

Date: 3/ 10 / 01
To: DPA
          Heilsbuch 2
          D-5122 Bonn
Re: Dt. Psychologentag
Job #:   nw 8038
Our i.d. #: 23-412 2323

DESIGN & ART DIRECTION

         1. design $10.00

         2. FedEx $73.32

                 Total $83.32
8.25% tax of all taxable items
            Grand total $83.32

karlssonwilker inc.
536 6th avenue
2nd & 3rd floor
new york city 10011
212 929 8064
fax 929 8063
www.karlssonwilker.com

our fast-made letterhead, fax sheet, and early invoice. Our database became one of the most important things in the

karlssonwilker inc.

536 6th avenue
2nd and 3rd floor
new york, ny 10011

jan wilker

t 001 212 929 8064
f 001 212 929 8063
tellmewhy@karlssonwilker.com

karlssonwilker inc.

536 6th avenue
2nd and 3rd floor
new york, ny 10011

hjalti karlsson

t 001 212 929 8064
f 001 212 929 8063
tellmewhy@karlssonwilker.com

karlssonwilker inc.

536 6th avenue
2nd and 3rd floor
new york, ny 10011

the intern

t 001 212 929 8064
f 001 212 929 8063
tellmewhy@karlssonwilker.com

karlssonwilker inc.

536 6th avenue
2nd and 3rd floor
new york, ny 10011

t 001 212 929 8064
f 001 212 929 8063
tellmewhy@karlssonwilker.com

Welcome to Portfolio Island.

HI DEARS

Wenn das "halo" ein "hallo" wäre, dann würde "I wish you a merry Christmas" bedeuten "Ich wische dich in Maria's chriesi mues!" Cheers.

Martin Woodtli, Designer

And we had T-shirts and sweatshirts made for us, our friends, and potential clients.

The redesigned Anne Klein lion. The client said, "You have never even seen a person that belongs to our target group. That's why we need you." (70)

DECIPHERING THE OFFICE (I):

WHISKEY IN PLASTIC BOTTLE - A GIFT FROM A PRINTER
BACKYARD ROOFTOP
SPONGEBOB
STONE STREET TAVERN MUGS
CLEANING SUPPLIES BEHIND THIS DOOR
SMALL PLANT. USED TO BE SMALLER
RIGHT SPEAKER
LIGHT BEHIND THE MIRROR
A NEW PLASTIC JESUS LIGHT

OUR INTERNS SIT HERE
BIG FIRE DOOR - WE ALWAYS KEEP IT OPEN LIKE THIS
FAXPRINTERCOPIER - IS CONNECTED TO THE IMAC
THE BIG HUSKY TOOLBOX
THE BACKSTREET BOYS BATTERY-POWERED POSTER - PLAYS 1 SONG ("GET DOWN")
GREY WOODEN FLOOR. DOWN BELOW IS DUNKIN' DONUTS
PORTFOLIO ISLAND (SIDE VIEW)
DISCO BALL - BIRTHDAY GIFT FROM JAN TO HJALTI
SPRINKLER - MOST LIKELY TOO OLD TO WORK
THIS IS WHERE THE LITTLE 99 CENT PLASTIC JESUS LIGHT WAS PLUGGED IN.
JAN'S LITTLE "NAD" AMPLIFIER. HE HAD IT SENT OVER FROM GERMANY.
HJALTI'S CELLPHONE (JAN STILL HAS NONE)
THE OFFICE OF PAUL SAHRE IS ABOVE THIS SPACE
ELECTRIC RODENT REPELLER. MIRACULOUSLY, IT WORKS.
6TH AVENUE
HJALTI, SITTING
BUZZER
GARBAGE CANS. THEY HAVE PRINTED MEASURING UNITS ON THE SIDE.
JAN, SITTING
ENGLISH/ICELANDIC DICTIONARY
OFFICE CLOCK
T-SQUARE PLACEMENT
PLANTS. THEY USED TO BE BIGGER.
LITTLE HUSKY
ENTRANCE DOOR
LIGHT

89

THE SOFA. FOR CLIENTS AND AFTERNOON NAPS
THE LOG WAS ALREADY IN THE OFFICE WHEN WE MOVED IN
THE CABINET WAS ALSO LEFT BEHIND BY PREVIOUS TENANTS
CARPET WITH STAINS
BOOKS
COMFORTABLE CHAIR
THE SOFA CRACK

Another restaurant we did, this time in downtown Manhattan's Financial District. All signage and goldleaf on the back were flipped. The client requested a "conservative place with a twist." (71)

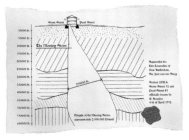

This fictitious map is from our first presentation, showing the location of The Moving Stone.

DEAREST CUSTOMER,

YOU ARE IN FRONT OF THE BACK OF OUR LOVELY TAVERN. JUST WALK AROUND THE CORNER AND YOU WILL FIND YOURSELF IN FRONT OF THE HISTORIC STONE STREET TAVERN.

— Welcome —

96 GESTURES   SCOTT FIELDS ENSEMBLE

CARRIE BIOLO, VIBRAPHONE. STEPHEN DEMBSKI, CONDUCTOR. SCOTT FIELDS, ELECTRIC GUITAR. FRANÇOIS HOULE, CLARINET. ROBBIE LYNN HUNSINGER, OBOE, ENGLISH HORN. JOSEPH JARMAN, ALTO SAXOPHONE, Eb FLUTE. ROB MAZUREK, CORNET. MYRA MELFORD, PIANO. JASON ROEBKE, DOUBLE BASS. DAMON SHORT, DRUM KIT. HANS STURM, DOUBLE BASS. MATT TURNER, CELLO. DYLAN VAN DER SCHYFF, DRUM KIT

BLUESHIFT CRI

BARCODE 0-90438-20012-7

96 GESTURES

SCOTT FIELDS ENSEMBLE

1. PERFORMANCE 2 TIME: 68:54. CD 2. PERFORMANCE 4 TIME: 66:57. CD 3. PERFORMANCE 5 TIME: 62:26 RECORDED LIVE IN THREE TAKES WITH:

TOTAL PLAYING TIME OF ALL THREE DISCS: 3:18:17 ℗&© 2001 COMPOSERS RECORDINGS, INC. 73 SPRING STREET, SUITE 506, NEW YORK, N.Y. 10012 PHONE (212) 941-9673 WWW.COMPOSERSRECORDINGS.COM (CRI LOGO) (BLUESHIFT LOGO) CD 2001 DDD (COMPACT DISC LOGO) THE BARCODE IS LOCATED ON THE SPINE

BLUESHIFT CRI

96 GESTURES

SCOTT FIELDS ENSEMBLE

BARCODE 0-90438-20012-7

REFLECTION ON KARLSSONWILKER
AND ON HJALTI AND JAN

I certainly was happy to be able to work at such
a great firm with two very talented designers,
though not sure how much 'talented' means
coming from a nobody designer—me...hee

what is talent?
if talent is being free and open and dedicated
yes, I see that in them
they smack each other on the head,
they wrestle, they groove to the Backstreet Boys

they sit for hours working on projects,
sleep over at the office sometimes,
they work hard and party hard,
work hard even on days when they come in with
a hangover,
party hard even on days when they've worked
for 18+ hours straight,

they may appear idle or playing, but actually
are pondering for solutions,
it is a firm that allows for creative explorations

it's a very "guy-ish" working environment
constantly dogging/mocking/putting down each
other,
the male ego trying to prove himself better
than the other,
too bad I'm not the ultimate prize that they
are trying to win over
(ha ha ha)

juxtapositions, the firm is filled with that
techno to Backstreet Boys
manliness to boyishness
machismo to sensitivity
seriousness to goofiness
clean chic to industrial...

all these make them the more unique and
individualistic free talented
designers as people can be

it was certainly a great experience working there
Hjalti and Jan, ready to take me back?

Jean Lee, Designer
(and a former intern at karlssonwilker inc.)

98

Another CD for the CRI/Blueshift series. We got a kick out of starting the type on the spine and going to the back. (74)

1.BLUEGREENYELLOW (10.01)
DAVID LIEBMAN, TENOR SAXOPHONE (BLUE)
ELLERY ESKELIN, TENOR SAXOPHONE (GREEN)
RICK DIMUZIO, TENOR SAXOPHONE (YELLOW)
JOHN HOLLENBECK, DRUMS/LAUGHTER SAMPLES
2.WITHOUT MORNING (4.21)
THEO BLECKMANN, VOICE
BEN MONDER, GUITAR
JOHN HOLLENBECK, PERCUSSION
3.LIEBMAN / HOLLENBECK VIGNETTES (6.33)
SIX IMPROVISED DUOS
DAVID LIEBMAN, TENOR SAXOPHONE
JOHN HOLLENBECK, DRUMS / PERCUSSION
4.THE DRUM MAJOR INSTINCT (24.59)
RAY ANDERSON, TROMBONE
DAVID TAYLOR, TROMBONE

TIM SESSIONS, TROMBONE
JOHN HOLLENBECK, DRUMS / PERCUSSION
DR. MARTIN LUTHER KING, JR., VOICE ON TAPE
5.ESKELIN / HOLLENBECK VIGNETTES (6.57)
SIX IMPROVISED DUOS
ELLERY ESKELIN, TENOR SAXOPHONE
JOHN HOLLENBECK, DRUMS / PERCUSSION
6.NO IMAGES (4.30)
JOHN HOLLENBECK, AUTOHARP WITH PORTABLE FAN

TOTAL PLAYING TIME: 57.41 ℗&© 2001 COMPOSERS RECORDINGS, INC. 73 SPRING STREET, SUITE 505, NEW YORK, N.Y. 10012 UNITED STATES OF AMERICA PHONE 212.941.9673 WWW.COMPOSERSRECORDINGS.COM

blueshift

CD
2001
DDD

cri

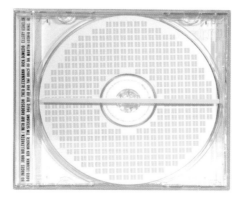

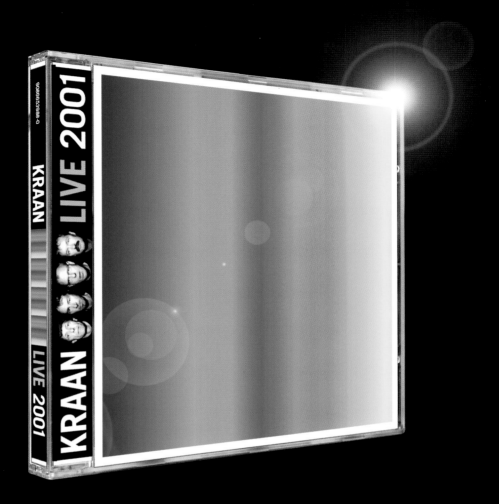

The perfect project to try some Adobe Illustrator® presets and swatch libraries.
CD and tour poster for Kraan. (74)

KRAAN
LIVE

PETER WOLBRANDT g/v JAN FRIDE d HELLMUT HATTLER b INGO BISCHOF k CD KRAAN LIVE 2001 BAS 20013 EDEL/CONTRAIRE

WWW.KRAAN.DE

getgo.de

102

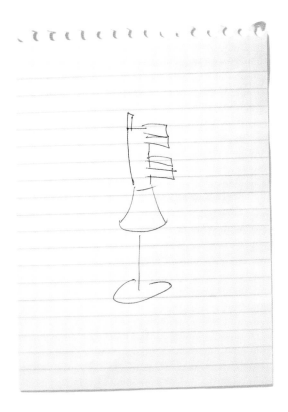

The dog lamp for World Studio Foundation. Still one of our favorite projects, although we forgot why. We made this sketch especially for this layout. (76)

The CRI/Blueshift projects were our playground.

These are the last CDs of the series. (77)

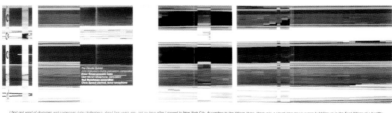

I first got wind of drummer and composer John Hollenbeck about five years ago, not so long after I moved to New York City. According to the Village Voice, there was a smart new music scene bubbling up in the East Village at a healthy distance from the well-established Capital D. Downtown scene centered around the Knitting Factory – and Hollenbeck was somewhere near the center of it.

One night early in the band's run, a woman named Claudia came forth from the throng to profess her ardent admiration for the band. "She rambled on and on about how she was going to make our gig a regular thing – she was going to tell all of her friends," Hollenbeck recalls. "When she was done captivating me with her good intentions, Reuben and I sauntered up to our instruments for the next set. He softly whispered to me, 'She's never coming back.'" Radding's premonition proved accurate – the Refuseniks never saw Claudia again. "We tried to continue the relationship with casual flibs," Hollenbeck says, "like, 'Hey, I saw Claudia on the street,' or 'Claudia left me a message that she is definitely rushing this week.' But Claudia maintained her absence. Eventually, Radding joined her, abandoning New York in pursuit of higher education.

Surprisingly, Claudia joined the new band as well, as its namesake and resident muse. "I called the group the Claudia Quintet in homage to Reuben," Hollenbeck says, "and I also wanted the group to have a sensitive, feminine quality." He hoped to downplay his leadership, in order to emphasize the ensemble. Since he intended to have the band play fully notated works as well as improvisations, Hollenbeck also saw in the name a parallel to the conventions of chamber music ensembles like the Arditti Quartet. Whether intentional or not, Claudia lent yet another quality to her namesake – a slippery sort of elusiveness that makes the band impossible to pin down and define. Is the Claudia Quintet a jazz band? A chamber ensemble?

"Burt and Ken" is one of the first pieces Hollenbeck wrote for the quintet. The title is a clever twist on the names of its two real-life dedicatees. The two distinct characters are sketched as deftly as Florestan and Eusebius, Schumann's compositional ego and id. "... after a dance, we have a pint with Gil and Tim..." refers to Gil Evans, who inspired the pastel modal vibraphone and military drum patterns of the second section, and Tim Berne, whose angularity is echoed in the first section. Hollenbeck refers to **"No D"** as a "Bruxtonish prog-funk ditty," proving that even at its brainiest, he intends the music to be fun for both player and listener.

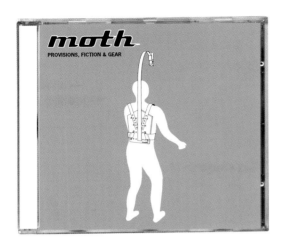

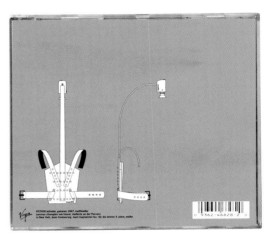

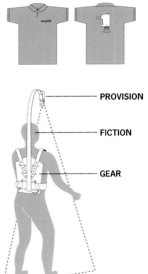

We got this project through our opening announcement. The record company liked our first presentation. The band did not.

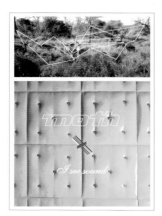

The band was still not happy.

108

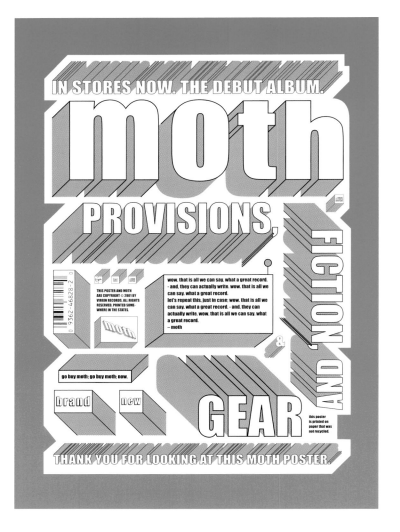

Here we got a bit desperate.

SKITCH HENDERSON - A Life in Music

Skitch Henderson is a one-man celebration of twentieth-century American music. Born in 1918 in Birmingham, England, with the name Lyle Russell Cedric Henderson, Skitch went on to successfully transform himself into a popular American icon and, in doing so, has managed to be at the center of every phenomenon in American popular music and culture. He began his career playing piano in the roadhouses of Montana and Minnesota in the 1930's and since then Skitch has been closely involved in all branches of popular musical entertainment. Live performances, movies, television, radio — Henderson has done it all, and all his work shines with his own

Skitch Henderson's big break came in 1937 when he filled in for an ailing accompanist for an MGM promotional tour featuring Judy Garland and Mickey Rooney. "The tour was to promote a film called Andy Hardy, which became a picture series," says Henderson. "Mickey's father was Joe Yule, the burlesque comedian, and Mickey 'cleaned up the act,' as we say. He did a monologue and I played something and Judy sang a couple of songs, and basically, we told everyone how wonderful MGM was." The tour started in Denver and wound up in Chicago, whereupon Skitch was left with the original pianist's roundtrip ticket to Hollywood. "It was like a scene from a Warner Brothers movie," says Skitch with a laugh. "The tour manager s
to do?' and I said I don't know and he said, 'Well I got a ticket, why don't you come to Hollywood?' And that's exactly how I went."

Once in Hollywood, Skitch continued playing piano however he could. He accompanied a young vocalist named Dolores Reed (the future Mrs. Bob Hope), joined the music department at MGM, and ultimately played piano for Bob Hope and The Pepsodent Show. "Bob and Dolores are like family to me," says Henderson. "Just like Bing. In fact, it was a
The reference is to Bing Crosby, of course, who went on to play an important role in Skitch's life. "He was like a guru for me," says Skitch. "Bing taught me stage presence and manners; he taught me a great deal. He was an incredible human being." Crosby was also instrumental in creating Skitch's nickname. As Henderson explains it, "I was called 'the sketch kid' because of the way I would quickly sketch out a new score in a new key. And Bing said, 'If you're going to compete, get your name straightened out. People always forget Christian names but they never forget nicknames.'" Skitch laughs and adds, "And it was sage advice. Skitch really stuck. And I even changed my passport."

Welcome to Kinko's, found in Hjalti's garbage can and definitely a low point. (141)

THIS IS WHAT I CAME UP WITH

When I first met Hjalti and Jan, their eagerness to learn was apparent. Being young and having no experience running a business, not to mention an American company with all its tax and financial complexities, they were ready to hear every word I had to say.

I started explaining everything to them from how to record a transaction to retirement and tax planning. Though they listened intently, I knew the sheer volume of the information confused them. Over the years, however, I believe the young entrepreneurs have grown tremendously in the manner in which they do business. I am certain that their success will continue and they will be as large a contributor to the business community as they are to the graphic design circle.

More importantly, from day one until today, I have felt that they have always been kind, polite, and honest people. Hjalti and Jan are more than just good designers and good businessmen. They are good people.

Wayne Schwaeber, Accountant
P. Richard Schwaeber, P.C.

book II

Welcome To Color

this goes out to the few youngsters who are not yet sure about studying design or who are, but their parents need to be convinced:

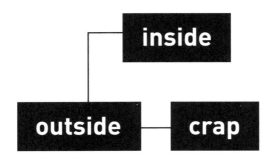

TINY STORIES (6):

this morning when i woke up i was surprised to find a colorful dampness on the pillow beside me. the roof did not leak and i could not find the source of the mysterious substance. later that day while delivering my presentation i noticed that the entire conference room seemed to be filled with the stuff. can anyone else see that, i asked. they didn't seem to understand that my question was unrelated to my research. it is quiet now and i am somehow ashamed.

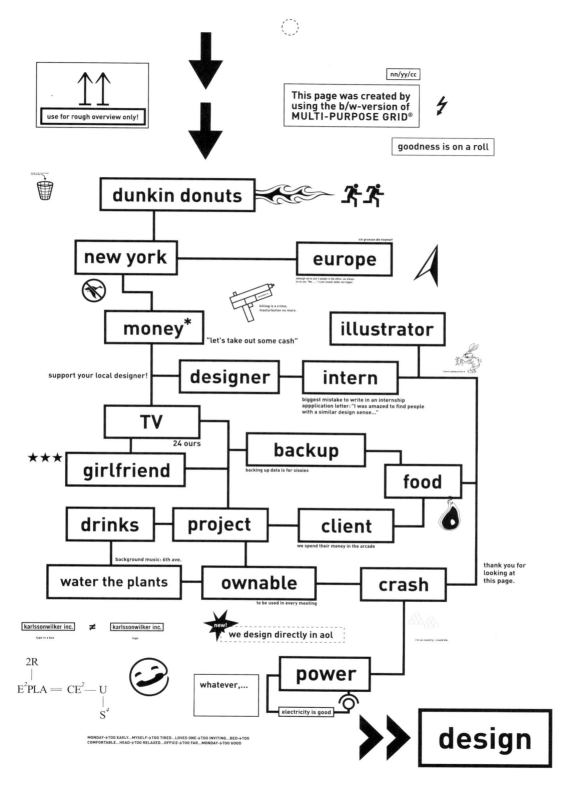

earlier today in a parallel universe:

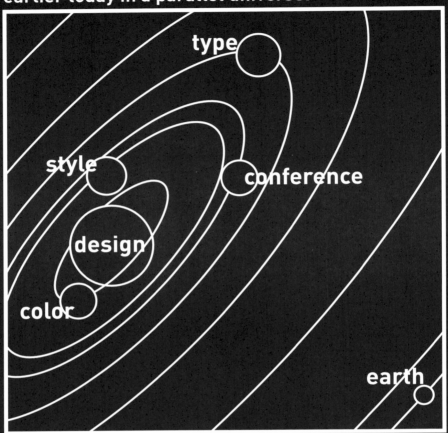

Behind the Scenes (1):

Meeting with a client:

client: so what we want is maybe this, did you ever do a 44.25" x 3.5" poster?

designer: ah, no. but sounds interesting.

client: hem, so you're telling me you have no experience at all in this design field...

last night in ny:

hello america: superlatives are the worst!

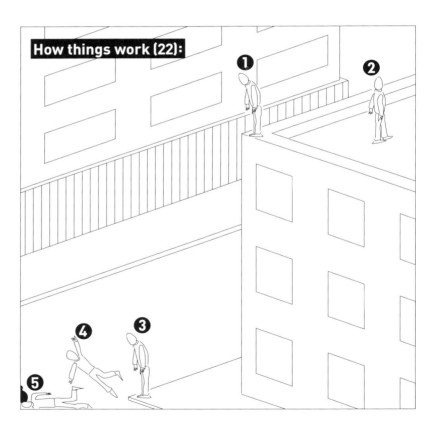

THIS IS NEW! THE UNBEATABLE CUSTOMER SERVICE:

INTERACTION WITH ANOTHER HUMAN BEING

BEND DOWN, GET AS CLOSE AS YOU CAN TO YOUR OPPONENT'S HAND. THEN TURN INTO AN
AXE AND CRACK HIS HEAD OPEN, DRAW A PEACE SIGN IN THE SAND, WATCH THE SUNSET,
AND GO HOME. ALL THIS IS BULLSHIT, BECAUSE THERE IS NO OPPONENT, NO AXE, NOT EVEN
YOU. IT'S ALL IN YOUR HEAD.

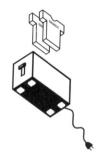

TINY STORIES (8):

once, when i was very young, a stranger asked me into his car. he
did not offer candy, but something about him led me to believe
that he could be trusted. my mom said that i shouldn't ride with
strangers. that's okay, he grumbled, she is probably just afraid that
you will usurp her as the new prince of toy kingdom. what's that, i
asked. you don't know about toy kingdom. sheesh. you are one
dumb kid. then he drove off. when i asked my mom about toy
kingdom, she just bowed her head and cried.

DESIGNING IN

LUNCH IS IMPORTANT. IT FEEDS T
FRESH IS THE ONE AND ONLY GOA
BUT NEVER LOOK AT DESIGN ANN
ONLY HURTS YOUR VERY OWN DESI
YOUR EYES. PICTURE A BUTTERF
CLOSED. OPEN THEM NOW. SLOW
AND ALWAYS REMEMBER: ART IS A

see you in hell.

EATABLE CUSTOMER SERVICE:

E NEW MILLENNIUM

RAIN. YOU'LL GET NEW IDEAS. FRESH. YES. STAYING
VER REPEAT, NEVER RIP-OFF; REFERRING IS FINE,
, DESIGN BOOKS; PUT THESE MAGAZINES AWAY. IT
NSE. SUBCONSCIOUSLY. THE DEVIL IS VISUAL. CLOSE
CORPORATE COLORS ARE ALLOWED. KEEP THEM
THING CHANGED. WELL DONE! YOU'RE NOT DEAD.
ER SOURCE FOR STEALING ANYWAY.

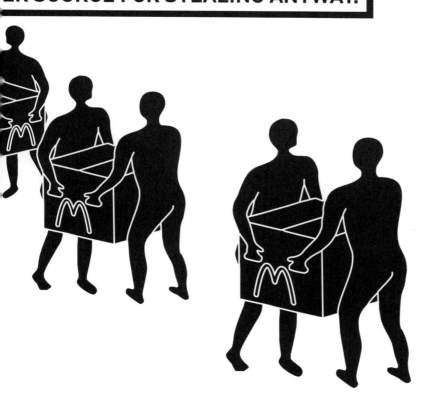

Behind the Scenes (2):

Meeting with a fellow designer:

fellow designer: how's business?

designer: ah, well, o.k., maybe a
little slow, but, no, we're
actually pretty busy right now.
we might do this big project
soon, but, no, everything is
great here.

fellow designer: hey, good for you, I
mean, same here, ah.

TINY STORIES (9):

i walk three miles to school everyday. and back. and everyday the thought goes through my head that one day i will tell my grandchildren about this walk. they will laugh at me as they ride by in their hoverbikes. they will think i am lying. even in the freezing rain, i will say, just like the postman. but they won't even have postmen. they'll have telepathy or some shit. they'll look at me like i am some crazy old coot. i'll rub my whiskers and sigh. in my mind i will be walking the same goddamn walk i am now.

THIS IS NEW! THE UNBEATABLE CUSTOMER SERVICE:

THE DEVIL HAS ALL THE GOOD TUNES

AAAAAAAAAAAAAAAAAAAAAAAAAAAAAAAAAAAAAAAAAAAAAAAAAAAAAAAAAAAAAAAAAAAAAAAAAAAAAAA
AAAAAAAAAAAAAAAAAAAAAAAAAAAAAAAAAAAAAAAAAAAAAAAAAAAAAAAAAAAAAAAAAAAAAAAAAAAAAAA
AAAAAAAAAAAAAAAAAAAAAAAAAAAAAAAAAAAAAAAAAAAAAAAAAAAAAAAAAAAAAAAAAAAAAAAAAAAAAAA
AAAAAAAAAAAAAAAAAAAAAAAAAAAAAAAAAAAAAAAAAAAAAH!

a new typeface is born: **ABÇąbç123**

defendant: i didn't know the gun was loaded.

exhibit A: i didn't know the defendant was loaded.

Great Designers are made, not born.

The Better Design Video Series®

Over Four Million Sold!

2 FREE VIDEOS!
Advanced Oral Design Techniques, our free 30-minute video, is guaranteed to increase your design-making pleasure. Great Design 7 Days A Week shows you even more creative ways to ignite intense design excitement.

Interspersed with explanations and advice from nationally recognized design therapists, each video features explicit design scenes of everyday couples sharing their most intimate and passionate moments. Listen to what they say. Watch what they do. And then set off on your own design journey.

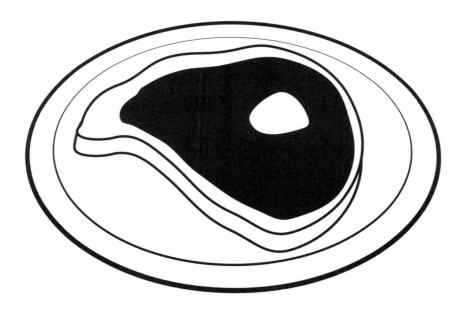

When I saw all these images of these starving kids in africa,
I just had to react in a personal way, so I drew this steak for them.

TINY STORIES (10):

i don't know if i have ever been as bored as when i sat in on dad's trial. i mean, the lawyers just kept talking and talking. occasionally they pointed at me. i figured this was the time when i was supposed to look pathetic, but i don't know if it came across right. i had to wear a suit and it was itchy. also, there was some old woman on the jury who kept looking at me like i was lunch. anyway, dad got off scott free and now i get to live with him. i'd be upset but he lets me drink and says i can screw girls if i want.

THIS IS NEW! THE UNBEATABLE CUSTOMER SERVICE:

GARDENING WITH OSCAR DE LA RENTA

"I LOVE ALL BEETS!" WOW. WHAT ELSE CAN WE ADD TO THIS? SO LET'S TALK ABOUT SEXUAL ABUSE: 34% OF ALL FEMALES WILL GET SEXUALLY ABUSED BEFORE THEIR 18TH BIRTHDAY BY THEIR FATHERS, STEPFATHERS, OR WHOEVER WALKS BY. MAYBE THERE IS NOT MUCH TO TALK ABOUT, MORE TO ACT. BUT WE DON'T KNOW ANY CASE OF SEXUAL VIOLENCE, LET ALONE DOMESTIC. WELL, NOT IN OUR NEIGHBORHOOD. AND WHAT HAS ALL THIS TO DO WITH DESIGN? NOTHING. JUST SOME MORE COPY IN BOXES. SAY THANKS TO YOUR MOM AND DAD FOR BEING THERE FOR YOU. AND A MAN HAS TO DO WHAT A MAN HAS TO DO, RIGHT? SO LET'S GARDEN.

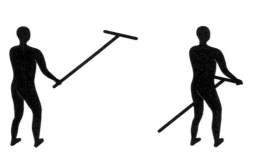

THIS IS NEW! THE UNBEATABLE CUSTOMER SERVICE:

ONE WORD IS ENOUGH FOR ALL OF US

YOUR NEIGHBOUR IS AT WORK. YOU ARE GOING THROUGH HIS FILES. HIS WIFE IS IN EXCELLENT SHAPE. HE DOESN'T DESERVE HER. SHE KNOWS. ARE YOU A GUY IN THIS STORY? CAN ANYONE EXPLAIN? THANKS. I'M OFF. RIDING ON MY ASSHOLE NEIGHBOR'S BACK. WHICH IS — COOL.

we know it's a little late, but we just had to...

our contribution to terror design:

desllgNY

see

UN-JOIN THE G.A.G. TODAY!

Story continued from page 80

Can't Live without Them.

Friendship is a constant theme at karlssonwilker—friends in business, friends on the sofa, friends at the door. When Hjalti and Jan talk about the many friends who become their clients, what sounds like shame often creeps into their voices—it seems to them that only people who know them will hire them. But maybe this is admirable. People like them for more than their social graces or their expertise at PlayStation. They might see them at a party one night, yet have enough respect for them in the morning to call them with work. And working with friends can be fun—no formal meetings or follow-up phone calls are required.

That voice of shame might come from the fact that friendship sometimes clouds their judgment. When their friend Alastair Bell comes to them with a dubious job, it sounds like just what they need. Alastair is the production manager of a company with the obliquely Orwellian name General Strategic Marketing. GSM is a group of middlemen who bring established companies together with designers who can update their identities. It has made a pitch to the New York Pops, and when they accept it, GSM makes another to karlssonwilker. Sure, the job is only a press release, but this can lead to more work—a new logo, new letterhead, who knows how many jobs and how much money? After twenty hours of meetings and fifteen proposals, the job goes nowhere. Jan writes up an invoice for $200, and GSM pays it four months later.

When Hjalti and Jan look back on this job, they try to find a lesson in it. They certainly learned nothing about design, as there was little design involved. They might have learned how to act in meetings, or how to trust their instincts when they sense that a job is nonsense, or that a small job will never lead to something big. But when they think of the same mistakes they make today, they are not sure they have learned anything.

The final August job is the one that breaks Jan's heart. It comes from one of his best friends in New York, Katie Liu. She heads Staff International, a New York office that owns several popular clothing labels, including D^2, Diesel Style Lab, and New York Industries. She asks Jan and Hjalti to design a postcard that Staff can use as announcements for fashion shows, invitations for parties, and the like. She will pay them well in both money and designer clothes, and this is exactly what the pair need right now. They are in bad financial shape. Without cash, they have not bought themselves new clothes in a year, except for the pair of suits for the ill-fated mailer photo.

Jan meets with Katie a few times at her office. The Staff staff is nice, and Jan appreciates that his friend has brought him into her fun fashion world. He especially enjoys picking out the four $300 sweaters and the single pair of $200 jeans that are part of the payment. (Jan jokes that since the clothes are all model sizes, only he can fit into the jeans.) And the postcard is good work. He plays with the colors and logos until he is satisfied. But he never finishes off the files for Katie. No matter how many times he talks about this job (and he talks about it often), he cannot

129

figure out what blocked him from completing it. Katie and Jan remain friends, but to this day they have never discussed what went wrong. She never asks about it, and he never has to come up with excuses for it. Karlssonwilker kept the clothes, and Staff kept its money. It remains Jan's biggest job-related regret.

Another friend offers dry goods to help karlssonwilker during its rough spell. Robert Wong gives the office the library from his defunct dot-com company. Over 400 books and magazines—design titles like *Power Packaging*, *The New Big Book of Logos*, and *Successful Methods of Marketing, Guaranteed!*, as well as general titles that somehow made their way into the dot-com library like *The Wonders of Life*, *Optics: The Science of Vision*, and *Predicting the Future*—are not exactly the kind of thing the studio can use. (Karlssonwilker's library instead consists of books like *Catch 22*, *The 100 Best Films to Rent You've Never Seen*, and *Die Geschichte der Kunst*.) But they are grateful for the gift. They decide to sell the books to a nearby used-book store, but suspect that they will get more money if they sell them off a few at a time, so every few weeks they gather up an armful and trudge around the corner. They could put this money toward office supplies or utility bills, but a gift is a gift, and they plan to use it as one. They put each dollar in a glass jar to save up for a $500 foosball table, which they have already picked out.

Yes, the partners are dreaming of foosball while Hjalti's girlfriend is paying all his personal expenses and Jan is sleeping on the office floor. Scrimping for every penny—cutting back on Hjalti's Coke habit and Jan's cigarettes—puts them in an increasingly bad mood. So every once in a while they go crazy, charging an expensive dinner or blowing $80 on a night of pool. They waste money on scratch-off lotteries, hoping that Hjalti's big win might repeat itself. Their story is not as simple as "they have no money so they have no fun." They are only human, and so not strictly logical. In theory they would prefer that when they spend money recklessly they do so for their friends—maybe a dinner party for all the people who have brought them work, or some small gifts for their long-suffering girlfriends. But their erratic habit is their little secret, a private fix they can only share with each other.

The happy couple is split up for one week at the end of August. Janet Froelich, art director of the *New York Times Magazine* (and a friend of a friend of a friend), is short-staffed from all the summer vacations and phones karlssonwilker for some help. They decide Jan will do the work, laying out Quark files according to the *Times* template. He is not used to such text-heavy design, but he does not find it too difficult. And because he knows Photoshop, he takes some more interesting jobs from the Quark-only regulars on staff. For his first freelance job ever, $1,200 is not bad money. It will help karlssonwilker stay afloat for another month. He should be happy with the nine-to-five program. But all the time he is sitting behind a midtown computer, he realizes how much better it is to be at karlssonwilker. There is just no going back after owning your own office. He does not mind when the magazine does not offer him more work.

Yorkers, just continue to keep themselves busy with work.

They are committed enough to karlssonwilker to think again about promoting it. Friends and clients have been bugging them for months to update their Website, and they now have enough work to post something substantial. They also have enough free time to devote to it, although you could argue that they have had this free time for months. So they replace the simple "we do design" with a complex combination of elements. There is, of course, their portfolio, the only color element on the site. There is also a short film of a man attacked by his own shoelaces; Jan made this during his student days. There is a man who scratches his butt when you touch him with your cursor. When you click on "jobs," you are sent to an application for employment with McDonald's. When you click on "how things work," a diagram shows you how to breathe.

All of this is set up as a kind of animated version of karlssonwilker's mailer; in fact, it duplicates some of their favorite illustrations. Hjalti and Jan make a conscious decision not to design a flashy Website with vibrant color, three-dimensional images, and motion. Their site reflects their work and their attitude. (Type in "karlssonwilker" on most search engines, and the description "24/7 design pimpin'. bigtime." follows the company's Web address.) They hire their friend Francisco Castro to program the site and pay him $1,500, which is a big amount for them and a small amount for him. But he is happy to work on such an unusual project and for the break in his routine.

Hjalti and Jan are thrilled with their new site. They decide they need to promote it so that other people will see it. They consider designing a postcard but instead make another newsprint piece to mail to friends and potential clients. Halfway through the endeavor, they ponder how strange it is to create an analog promotion for a digital project. They print five hundred copies anyway, then discover that they have misspelled "how to breathe" as "how to breath." Still, they send out two hundred of these, after grading them with a big A- in red pen. The rest sit in shame in a corner of the office.

Keeping Up with the Culture.

The studio does not always sit around waiting for a friendly knock on its door. It does occasionally drop off its portfolio around town, and in October this leads to a meeting with VH1. Hjalti actually made the drop in July, but now he has waited long enough. He phones up Nancy Lee, vice president off-air creative, and she invites the duo to meet her at her office. VH1 asks karlssonwilker and two other firms for a paid pitch for its media kit: a binder of printed material as well as giveaways like video cassettes, posters, T-shirts, and hats. The network wants to use elements from the kit to update its business identity, and karlssonwilker suggests using them as a basis for a new ad campaign. Nancy and the other two women at the table like the idea. They also like karlssonwilker, but they are hesitant to work with a two-person firm. Who will be the project coordinator?

Hjalti and Jan decide to bring Rick Albert back into their lives. Surely he has enough experience to manage a complicated job like this. Rick is happy for the offer and brings along a writer named Carey Fox, whose resume is filled with fancy titles and big-name jobs. It looks like a complete team to take on VH1. But when Rick and Carey suggest "brainstorming," the designers question whether this foursome is in sync.

Hjalti and Jan listen to Carey's suggestions—tag lines like "hit list" and "stay tuned"—and find few of them interesting. They also listen to Rick's fatherly advice, "You guys should keep up with the culture," which they both find very amusing. Then the four plod through the work. They talk and talk and talk some more, and soon enough Hjalti and Jan realize that they have just two days to build all the mock-ups, set up all the photo shoots, and draw all the art they will present to VH1.

They develop two approaches to the job. One uses a tag line suggested by Carey, "off the charts." For this they draw up abstract graphs (some made into letterforms, others into complex three-dimensional models) and chart the more obscure data of the music industry, from the growth of hair bands to the length of guitar solos. Their proposal shows ways to place the graphs on various elements of the media kit. The other proposal uses VH1's existing tag line, "music first." The station has downplayed their motto over the past few years, and the designers suggest reviving it. For this approach they focus on the ad campaign and set up a photo shoot using the theme: a woman feeding her pregnant stomach with music, a burglar sorting through the CDs he is about to steal, a guy choosing just the right music while his lover pouts impatiently in bed, and the proud owner of a new car stereo system eyeing the new car he hopes to own someday. It is a fun day; they like playing photographer, and their friends like being models. Hjalti poses for one shot, and Vera for another. (Vera also helps out this month with some work from Anne Klein. The logo for Anne Klein Sport, a new athletic line, is a welcome job at the studio.)

Monday's date with VH1 arrives soon enough. Hjalti and Jan bring Rick along to help them present their designs. He is used to presentations like this, and he certainly got more sleep over the past two days than they did. Rick does most of the talking at the meeting, and it seems to go well. Still, it is a long wait before they hear from Nancy. When she does call, she tells them that VH1 likes the ad campaign they propose and might just use it someday. (They have not yet.) But they think the media kit is just too ordinary and corporate, and choose another firm to put it together. Hjalti and Jan suggest the three women at VH1 deemed their proposal too harsh and cold, not warm and feminine. More likely, in trying to please their corporate client, Hjalti and Jan gave up the noncorporate style that first interested VH1 in their work.

Hjalti wishes that VH1 would be memorable for more than "you guys should keep up with the culture." Sure, he still laughs at the line every time Jan throws it at him. But VH1 would be a great client. It is his primary job-related regret.

Repeat Customers.

It is October 2001, and the office is starting to show its age. A year of business is wearing down the office machines, and Hjalti and Jan learn that neither is very handy with them, if they do not know this already. First Hjalti throws out his "broken" cordless phone, only to realize that its batteries were dead. Then Jan spends $300 on a new drum and toner for the office's printer/fax/copy machine; five months later, when he discovers the machine's manual tucked into the Husky, he learns he only needed to clean its scanning module. Hjalti and Jan pay even less attention to their office supplies. They typically send out jobs in the packages in which the proposals came. And though it would be nice to say that they are being environmentally conscious, it is probably more accurate that they have neither the money nor the patience to order packing supplies. Their lack of concern produces a kind of aesthetic. Their railroad-track-print packing tape appears to be a well-considered anti-design statement, even if it is only a castoff from a friend.

At the end of the month, Tony Goldman calls with his third project for the firm. It is another restaurant in Philadelphia, this one downtown instead of out near the university. Hjalti and Jan visit the site on the ground floor of a nondescript office building, a typical four-story modern structure. It has "corporate" written all over it. Hopefully its high-end audience will appreciate their work more than the patrons of El Diner did. They do not want their design work to be flushed down the toilet again.

Tony already has a name for the restaurant, "Kitchen and Bar." But Hjalti and Jan are not sold on it. They know Tony well enough to know that he respects their opinions, so they question him on his choice, and he asks them to try out new names in their proposal. They come up with "Trust," "Soda," "Dolby," and "Traffic." He likes "Trust," with "A Kitchen and Bar" as its subtitle.

Tony wants full design services again, including signage, stationery, gift certificates, matchbooks, pins, and advertisements. Hjalti and Jan propose unifying the many elements with a single shade of green—green on the menus, green on the coasters, green on the building's columns, green on the rolls of toilet paper, even green water running from the faucets. Green is the color of money, which works well with the banklike facade of the restaurant, the name "Trust," the symbol of a handshake that the designers propose for the project's logo, and the charts they submit for the menu design.

Hjalti and Jan present this package to Goldman Properties. Tony is not available for the meeting, so their old friend Gary Farmer reviews the work without him. He takes their proposal back to his staff in Philadelphia and comes back with a list of words they think suit the restaurant better than karlssonwilker's "trust": "warm, simple, sincere, earthy, romantic, gentle, cozy, reassuring, established." This list means basically starting from scratch, and Hjalti and Jan are not prepared for this. Tony has always loved whatever they have presented him. They prefer their initial instincts for the project to Gary's Martha Stewart–like roster, but what can they do? To achieve the words Gary

135

wants, they ask him for photographs of the restaurant's interior, for which he is in charge—samples of the floor, sofa cover, and bathroom wall. They use these elements as backgrounds for a script font on a complete redesign. They put this together grudgingly but well, and set a date to meet with Goldman Properties again. This time Tony will be there.

Their instincts are right. Tony has already seen their initial proposal, the boards still sitting around his office, and much prefers it to the "warm" and "simple" model. He tells his staff that they should never ask karlssonwilker to start over. He knows they will not produce something as good as their first idea. Hjalti and Jan are flattered by this recognition. In just three projects, they have developed a great relationship with Tony, one of mutual respect. So when Tony critiques parts of their proposal, they do not even flinch. His suggestions for previous work have always made the project better. He is happy with the corporate look, but does not like the green band and the handshake. He loves the menu charts, but does not think they will work with the theme. Tony scraps them from Trust, but hopes to reuse them at a noodle house he is planning to open next door.

Hjalti and Jan come up with a new idea to symbolize "trust." They find a set of stock photos of trapeze artists holding each other in midair; each view is somehow sweet in its cheesiness. They paste these black-and-white scenes on background colors mimicking the restaurant's interior palette, and add text in a blocky font. When "trust" appears in this font in upper-case letters, it assumes a banklike demeanor. This is especially strong on the back-lit sign on the corner awning of the building.

The opening party for Trust is a love fest. Tony is thrilled with his new restaurant and tells Hjalti and Jan that they are now like family to him. They have had a few drinks by this time, so they readily return the sentiment. They let Tony know that his input made their design as good as it is. Two hundred people arrive to toast the evening. Somehow a photographer from *Philadelphia Weekly* focuses in on Hjalti and Jan and prints a picture of them huddled in a corner with their drinks. This is a prized moment, a record of a reprieve from a couple of bad jobs.

In November, Jan finally leaves his air mattress behind for a better apartment. He and Matthias (karlssonwilker's former couch resident and Stefan's new employee) take over Hjalti's place. Jan is a much happier man to wake up each morning on a real bed. After sharing a smoke with Matthias, he rides the bus to his office, and after a day of work he rides it home again, happy for the distance. Hjalti is still living at Vera's place and is glad to get some money to cover rent and utility bills for his otherwise unoccupied apartment. He sublet the place for a few months, but, now that his tenant is gone, he will have to reassume the fees. Now Jan and Matthias can help with this burden. Karlsson-wilker has seen enough work over the past couple of months to hope that it can afford this expense.

"This expense" means Jan's rent. That is, Jan's rent is an office expense. In their two years in business, Jan and Hjalti never got the $2500 per month salary they first conceived as "the minimum you can get by with in first months." In fact, they have never taken home any salary at all. Each month, when they review their office funds, they decide to write checks to the phone company and the messenger service instead of to themselves. And so Jan's rent and Hjalti's trips to Iceland and their slices from Mondello Family Pizza (now Soprano's) across the street get paid directly from their office account. It is a unique way to manage their money, and a sign of the seriousness of their partnership.

Karlssonwilker gets some work in November to keep the money rolling. It comes by way of Mary Fagot, the woman from Virgin with whom they had worked on the Moth project. She does not have a commission herself, but recommends them to Frances Pennington of DreamWorks Records. Frances asks them to design packaging for advance CDs to be sent to radio stations and reviewers. Because they will hold multiple bands, they need to be somewhat generic. Jan is in Germany, finally getting a chance to see Ella again and to recuperate from September in New York, so Hjalti works on the job alone. He has worked on many CDs, but this one does not come easily. DreamWorks has a conspicuous logo by Roy Lichtenstein, and it is difficult to incorporate into any design.

Hjalti prepares three proposals and is unhappy with all of them. DreamWorks is not too excited either. The job sits around for awhile, no one too eager to work on it or to have it done. When Jan returns, he tries his hand at it and comes up with two more schemes—again, nothing that DreamWorks is keen to use. After nine months of snail-paced action, the project seems stale to the studio. For karlssonwilker, the process starts to feel like editing, not designing. And Hjalti and Jan are not editors. A new intern, Daniel Pepice, adds some new life to the project, and with Jan produces something the studio really likes, made of diagonal lines and boxed texts. They propose that this be silkscreened in white on the jewel case, and that the liner be printed in different solid colors for each CD. Karlssonwilker likes to think that it never reuses a design, that it reacts to each project as an independent source for ideas. But there are clearly similarities between the DreamWorks proposal and the Blueshift series they designed for CRI, another job with a stamped case and individualized liner. This time, the color and black-and-white components are reversed.

DreamWorks is happy with this latest proposal and bids it out to a vendor. A few months later, the record company tells karlssonwilker that the silkscreening is too expensive to produce. It asks for a new, cheaper proposal. Someday Hjalti and Jan might just work on it. But for now, the DreamWorks design lives only on their Website.

Fall is bringing many repeat customers to karlssonwilker. Maybe the cool air is carrying a whiff of nostalgia along with it. More likely, people enjoy working with Hjalti and Jan, and once is not enough. Vera is their most faithful client. She is doing well at Anne Klein, but is overloaded with work. Why shouldn't her friends relieve some of her burden? The latest job is designing T-shirt motifs. Each one that is accepted pays $300, so Hjalti and Jan are happy to spend hours playing with type and color on screen. This is good work for their interns, too.

Another repeat customer is Constantin Boym, who arrives at their office with his second project. Encouraged by Hjalti and Jan, he uses the mailer they designed for him to pitch a book to Princeton Architectural Press about his souvenir project. The press likes the souvenirs, but knows Constantin has much more work to show and suggests publishing a monograph on all the designs produced by him and his wife, Laurene Leon Boym. Constantin is grateful to Hjalti and Jan, knowing that their mailer has led to this, and so proposes karlssonwilker as the book's designers.

Hjalti and Jan have to convince PAPress that they should do the job. They are not sure that this will be an easy task; even though Hjalti has worked on half a dozen books with Stefan, including Stefan's monograph, this will be karlssonwilker's first book on its own. Publishers often hesitate to hire designers without a few books in their portfolio. And record labels usually do not sign designers without CDs, clothing lines do not consider designers without finished pieces, etc. Hjalti and Jan are generally frustrated with this attitude. They think designers who only work on books or CDs or clothing can make some pretty boring stuff. Sometimes it is better to come to a project fresh rather than loaded with preconceptions and rules.

Constantin helps them with their proposal; he plans to be a significant participant in the book, not a client who sits back waiting for results. He chooses the trim size and the title, *Curious Boym*, based on the Curious George stories his son Bobby enjoys so much. Constantin likes how H. A. Rey's monkey discovers new things in his world and adapts them to his own use. This becomes the underlying theme of the project. The three men focus on the book's packaging in their design; Constantin is a product designer, so the volume should be a product. Hjalti and Jan consider making a book that can be converted into a lampshade, hang on the wall like a picture, or look like a laptop computer. Instead, they decide to cut a circular hole in the cover and then use the cut-away piece as a coaster at the book party. This works well with the adaptation theme of the book.

The collaborators discuss including inserts throughout the book, references to Constantin's fascination with materials. They debate a sheet of pressed flowers, one of sandpaper, and a spread of foil to be used for sunbathing. They also propose a page of Post-it stickers that readers can tear off to mark their favorite pages. They mock up all of these ideas for their meeting with PAPress and grab the portfolio that has been sitting idle for some time now. The pitch goes over well, and Hjalti and Jan begin to design the book on and off for the next seven months, then check proofs for two months. Compare this to their first job, seven weeks of design and production on Pat Metheny's *Trio–Live* CD for more money than *Curious Boym*, and it might seem like the design studio is working backwards.

But Hjalti and Jan enjoy this work. They do not consider all the time they spend in meetings or reviewing printouts or proofs a loss of money. Working with Constantin is just plain fun, more like a hobby or a game than work. He demands a lot of their time, insisting that they both be involved in every step of the project. But they know him well now and so never feel pressured by him. They can

138

get away with pranks, calling him in the middle of the project to say that they have lost all the files, or that he is the reason their partnership is breaking up. This is hilarious for a few minutes, until Constantin gets the joke and accuses them of childishness. He warns them that goofing around can look unprofessional and can keep them from big jobs. They worry that he is right.

The work goes along smoothly. The designers build a template that allows for the wide range of Constantin's designs. They make playful patterns out of the title's monogram and cover the endsheets with them. The only points of contention are the inserts. Some, like the sandpaper, are just too expensive to produce. And Hjalti, Jan, and Constantin decide that they should be more than just interesting materials: they need to relate to the chapters they introduce. The opener to the chapter called "Experiments" becomes an experiment gone wrong—"the worst pop-up ever done," in karlssonwilker's words. The next two inserts are more difficult to resolve. The three finally decide on a green shopping bag handle for the "Products" chapter and an empty blue room for the "Environments" section.

The final book is a success. Their experiments with materials pay off—you really can hold the book by its shopping-bag handle, and the coasters cut from the covers do their job at the book's opening party. The design is selected for the I.D. Annual Design Review. Best of all, Constantin is almost giddy with the final book. He will become a repeat repeat customer.

Who Are We and How Should We Behave?

Jan sits in his office, staring out the window. It is a cold New York day, and people are bundled up against the December weather. Many stop in the Dunkin' Donuts downstairs to warm up with some coffee. Jan is daydreaming of the holidays to come, the joy of spending time with his family around the *Tannenbaum*. But his itchy computer fingers interrupt this reverie. He wants to do something—this is why he is here. But karlssonwilker has no design work for him. Suddenly a vision of inspiration appears in his view. It is a sign, printed boldly on the service truck of a major telecommunications company. What a bold and dramatic logo it is! Jan is jealous, wishing his company had such a beautiful "z" in it. And then he realizes that with one simple stroke it can. A new logo for the design studio is born, all in five minutes. Hjalti is happy with Jan's design and not at all disturbed with the minor change to the spelling of his name in it. Karlzonwilker will proudly print this on their Christmas card next year. They are not at all concerned about a lawsuit.

The partners spend their holidays away from New York. Hjalti and Vera share a $25-a-night hotel room in Reno, skiing by day and feeding slot machines in the evening. Jan spends three weeks in Germany with Ella, highlighted by New Year's Eve playing roulette in Baden-Baden. All this gambling could make for a dramatic story—either the designers win a huge pot and save their fledgling company, or they lose their last penny and their business along with it. The truth is they drop no more than $100 a piece and return to their office as they left it.

Hjalti and Jan are happy to be back in the city. They add smiling photographs of themselves with their girlfriends to the pile stuffed into a little Husky drawer they have placed in the corner of the office. While their big Husky is filled with pens, clips, paper, FedEx folders, unused power cords and plant lights, lots of change (mostly pennies), a mini tape recorder, a "past due—please remit" stamp, and, for some reason, four pairs of sunglasses, its little brother houses only these photos, the office's private stash. One of their favorites is taken during a party to welcome their return. It shows them in a wrestling hold, arms and legs flailing, unclear who is on top of whom. Before this photo came a smaller fight, preceded by an even smaller fight, preceded by Jan smearing a Big Mac on Hjalti's shirt. The picture proves that they do not always get along. Or maybe it just proves that they get drunk together.

A different photograph of Hjalti and Jan graces the January issue of *Novum*, which finally runs the feature they put together in June. The journal tags karlssonwilker "pure design enjoyment from NY" and allows the studio to design its cover. Jan and Hjalti place the photo of themselves in their suits above the number .000000000324, explaining that "This decimal number comes from dividing 2 by the current figure for the world's population. It is thus a mathematical representation of two people on Earth"—and a clue as to how seriously they take their partnership. *Novum* redesigns their design, adding orange and yellow to the black-and-white proposal and stretching the text with odd word spacing. Still, karlssonwilker is happy for the free publicity and expects it to make their phones ring. They do get congratulatory calls from friends, but nothing from potential clients. The office gets some more publicity the next month, when Jarrett Kertez interviews the partners for reservocation.com. They especially appreciate his headline, which reads, "karlssonwilker inc. is making smart and quirky design fashionable again."

The winter brings more jobs from Anne Klein. The clothing company has developed a comfortable relationship with karlssonwilker. After their shaky start—Hjalti hesitating to work with his girlfriend, and Jan hesitating to sell himself in English to an important client. By now they have an easy routine. The players complete the jobs via phone and email, not even bothering with face-to-face interviews.

The first of four jobs is a pair of jacquards, one derived from the lion they redesigned as their first Anne Klein job, the other from the initials "AK." Hjalti and Jan present five proposals and get a flat fee of $3,000 for the two that are chosen. They ask for a buy-out fee of $8,000, knowing that these jacquards might get a lot of use, but Anne Klein will not include this in the contract. The second job is a stationery system for AK Anne Klein. For this, the designers use a show-through trick. They print the name and address on one side of the page and a red band on the other so that it appears like a pink band when seen through the paper. The third job is a new logo for Albert Nipon, a men's suit manufacturer owned by Anne Klein. They create a simple design using sans-serif type to be printed on a label. It will also be used as a new logo for the company, but Anne Klein pays less for a label than a logo, and so contracts it as such. The final job is for a new lion logo for Anne Klein's A Line. It is based on an American lion—the mountain lion—for an American clientele—shoppers at Wal-Mart and the like. The logo is never used, not because it is bad but because Anne Klein decides to stick to a text-based design. But this has no effect on the continuing partnership, and the exchange of relatively easy money. All four projects are small, designs done in bits and pieces, but they are important. Hjalti and Jan know that many more people will see their jacquards on a bag or belt than most of their other work.

A new intern works on some of the Anne Klein jobs. She comes to karlssonwilker on the recommendation of friends and works there two days a week. Hjalti and Jan like her, but not her work. (Despite her portfolio, they take their friends' recommendation.) She likes karlssonwilker, but is unsure about how she likes Hjalti and Jan. One day she tells Hjalti, "Jan is like a little puppy—sometimes he is so innocent and nice, and sometimes he can be so mean." After three months of mismatched design sensibilities, it is evident that the relationship is going nowhere. So Jan has to tell her that her internship is over. She cries and runs out of the office, banging the door after her (for which she later apologizes). If only the partners had trusted their instincts when they first viewed her portfolio, they would have evaded the whole problem.

Hjalti and Jan have a habit of giving every portfolio that comes to their office their full attention. No photographer, student, or designer who knocks on their door is too insignificant for their attention. They also respond to every query email, often times signing "David Carson" (people usually get the joke, and only one clueless student asks if he really works there). Most of the time, they are happy to see what other people are creating. But every once in a while they see portfolios—like that of the graphic designer who made the "A" in "PARIS" out of the Eiffel Tower—that just make them sad. The worst usually come from the weirdest people with the oddest stories and the greatest hopes for a collaboration.

Time Flies Very Slowly.
After the excitement of the *Novum* cover, it is a slow winter, moving into a slow spring, for the studio. There are a couple of highlights—a five-day vacation in Miami at one of Tony Goldman's hotels (Hjalti and Jan ask Tony for a good rate, and he gives them a couple of his best rooms for free). And Jan gives up smoking, which makes the fresh spring air that much sweeter. Other than that, it is business as usual. Hjalti gets a small job for the Icelandic Consulate. The work, an invitation for a conference in Los Angeles, includes little design. It is really just transcribing text, which he does quickly on a computer and prints at Kinko's. Hjalti welcomes it for its potential for more work for his homeland. But the job leads to nothing but an occasional call from their contact, who phones for social rather than professional reasons. And the Icelandic Consulate, Hjalti's hope for so much more, takes five months to pay its meager bill.

With business slow, the studio is happy to get a call from Stefan offering some freelance work. Stefan's employee (and Jan's roommate) Matthias is on vacation, and Stefan needs a hand. Hjalti and Jan enjoyed working with him, and they can certainly use the money, so they decide to help. Hjalti takes seven days and Jan two. Back in Stefan's office, both are amazed at how much they have changed. They have been self-employed for a year and a half now, and they find working for someone else difficult. Stefan gives them interesting projects, jobs that other designers would take on with enthusiasm. But they work half-heartedly, sitting in Stefan's office while missing their own. Finally they go home, paychecks in hand, and look forward to the next karlssonwilker job.

That job is for the SoHo Repertory Theater, a small local house showing unconventional plays. They get this work from their neighbor Paul Sahre, who has designed the theater's identity and several posters, and acts as the company's art director. Paul asks his friends to design their storefront window for an upcoming show. The work pays just $60 but gives the designers free creative range to fill the space as they like.

SoHo Rep sends karlssonwilker the script for its production, *Attempts on Her Life*. The show is taken from sixteen short stories, which the designers represent with sixteen laser pointers hanging from the ceiling. They send their latest intern, Jean Lee, to Chinatown to buy the lasers, and she manages to get them for just $56. This plus the black thread and pushpins to hang them up will come in just under their payment for the work. Jean sets up the pointers at the theater along with a simple sign relating to the theme of the stories, "The space behind this window was filled with mean thoughts on April 11th by a stranger." All in a day's work, the project is completed.

That is, until Paul comes knocking on the door. The theater is not happy with their design. They have installed their piece on top of the junk left over from the previous show. Is this what they meant to do? Hjalti and Jan do not know how to respond, as they have never seen their completed design. They thought it was a perfect job for an intern, and so left it all up to Jean. Paul is not so lackadaisical about the piece; he goes to the site and takes care of the trash himself.

There is another problem with the design. People have stopped by the window and expressed concern with its sign. They are especially affected by the "11th," seeing in it some veiled and disturbing reference to September 11th. SoHo Rep asks karlssonwilker to write up something new. Hjalti and Jan think this is all just too much. They refuse to make another sign, partly on principle and partly for the annoyance of the small job. The theater counters by refusing to pay their bill.

This is the studio's only bill that goes unpaid. While many small firms have trouble collecting their fees, karlssonwilker does not. This might have something to do with luck, or the fact that so many of their clients are friends. But it also has something to do with how they structure their relationships with clients. In its contracts, karlssonwilker insists on one-third payment up front. The initial payment is some indication that the designers can expect more. But their best guarantee to get paid is to not put in the lowest bid to get work. They have friends who decided they need to take low-paying jobs, only to find that low-paying usually means no-paying. Karlssonwilker might not get as much work as its cheaper competition, but at least it gets paid for the work that it does.

The slow spring is interrupted by a slow job. Dee Solomon refers Marie Regan to the studio. She wants to develop her own cosmetics line called "Piaffe." The name describes a horse's trotting in place and suggests a high-end clientele. Marie knows the value of good design, and she is looking for something special to promote her new line of fifty products. She knows a creative approach will incur a greater expense than a more simple design, but she understands that this is necessary. She plans to sell her lipsticks and eye shadows from a Website alone, and needs something to catch the browser's eye.

Hjalti and Jan are excited for the job and the opportunity to tackle some sophisticated work. They propose making the products unique by making the packaging, not just the logo on the packaging, unique. For this they cut a grid of circles into thin cardboard boxes, then line the boxes with a layer of foam. When the cosmetics are inserted into the package, they force the foam up through the holes, creating a singular texture. Marie loves this proposal; she knows it brings something special to her baby. She asks karlssonwilker to get prices and make a prototype of the idea, and the partners happily oblige. When the designers give Marie a high production estimate, she understands it as part of her high-end strategy.

A week later, the whole project turns around. Marie now thinks the production costs are too high. In fact, she has changed her mind about the entire conception of Piaffe. Instead of an elite line, with fifty products packaged in four-color boxes, it needs to be as inexpensive as possible, with only three products in boxes, and these in only two colors. Karlssonwilker cannot argue with her decision. They have invested only their design services in the project, and Marie will invest much more. They agree to start over, moving their work from packaging to logo design. It is a process they know well. They set a logo with a horse inside a circle above elongated type. Then they pattern multiple horses across a field to make an interesting pattern. This forms a simple filler, something more interesting than a solid color (they did this for the endpapers of *Curious Boym*, too). Marie is thrilled with their work. They are not. If they had accepted the commission as a logo job, they could be content with what they have done. But knowing that they have lost the opportunity to design more than a logo makes their revised work seem mediocre.

Piaffe is followed by another job for Anne Klein. The clothing company has been good to karlssonwilker, but they wish it would give them a big job, a major redesign, rather than the small projects that come along sporadically. April's job is another lion logo, the third karlssonwilker has designed for them. It is based on a three-dimensional lion-head buckle that Anne Klein found tucked away in its archives and wants flattened into a new logo. This is easy enough for Jan and Hjalti—take a picture, work some tracing software, and voila. It looks good, but the designers are not sure that it is ever used.

143

All the short days of winter give Hjalti and Jan serious spring fever. They lean back in their chairs, feet on their desks, and dream of summer. Maybe this year they can join Paul in a share in Montauk. Or maybe—why not?—they can take a more exotic vacation. Or maybe nothing will happen. Nothing seems to be happening. They seem to be, well, a little stuck. They need something big to get them back up again.

The First Big Job.
Hjalti and Jan know music CDs are good work for a design office; the designers can assume the cool of the artist as their own. But thus far their musician clients—Pat Metheny and the Blueshift artists—have not quite been the epitome of the celebrity cool. Their next, the Vines, is more what they have in mind, though no one knows at the beginning of the project just how cool—and big—they will become. Except for a couple of reviewers in the British press, no one outside of Australia has heard of the band in May 2002.

The Vines are brought to the office by Mary Fagot, who has left Virgin for Capitol. She asks Hjalti and Jan to design the group's *Highly Evolved* package. Mary enjoyed working with them on the Moth design. Though that project did not run its full course, she knows the designers have potential. They only have to convince Capitol's new CEO, Andrew Slater, that they have what Mary sees. They send him their portfolio, and he likes it well enough to send over the band's music and a couple of photos of the young and marketable band members. Hjalti and Jan like the CD, and tell Capitol that they love it. Hjalti recalls that he thought the band sounded like the Strokes. Jan recalls that he disagreed with Hjalti on this. Hjalti recalls that Jan did agree with him. And so it goes.

Capitol asks for a series of elements for the new release: packages for the album and singles, as well as advance CDs, posters, stickers, and such. Karlssonwilker comes up with two proposals, more for the sake of having two proposals than for any indecisiveness about their direction. One shows a dark purple, pixelated image with a square logo. The other, the one that will be sold on nearly half a million CDs (as of this writing), shows ecstatic red scribbles replacing the simple photos of the band members. Story continues on page 209

Our website launch announcement. After printing 500 of these, we noticed a typo in 1 of the 8 words. (133)

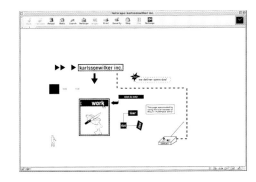

146

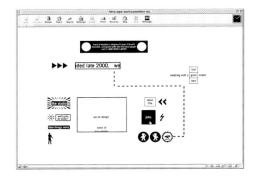

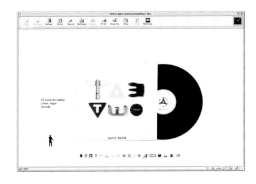

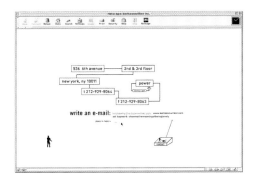

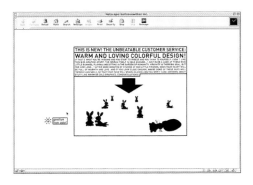

<Our website. In the first few months we showed a
few of Jan's old projects to fatten it up a little. (133)

KARLSSONWILKER = THINKING OUTSIDE THE BOX

Me, too. I wish I'd write in boxes . It seems to simplify the thought process. The little stories
karlssonwilker tells us, in black framed rectangles, are ordered itineraries of their crazy minds.
With each and every unnecessary step broken down into a box with arrows pointing around in random directions, their diagrams emulate the rational and often oversimplified information of design
vocabulary. Me, too. I could say, for instance, karlssonwilker = designers = great copywriters !
And I would mean it. The truth is: forget about the boxes, design is about thinking outside the box,
right (just to paraphrase another designer's motto)?

Karlssonwilker, in fact, has invented new mottoes: absurdist, self-deprecating, tongue-in-cheek.
The ad-like formulas that appear on their tabloid mailers echo the creative angst, the ominous
mental block, the "designer's nightmare," as they call it. They love to play the "artiste maudit,"
misunderstood by his time and clients. With karlssonwilker a new kind of self-promo is born: an
auto-celebration in reverse, mocking the laudatory sales speech, the pompous credentials of capa-
bility brochures, the corporate lifetime accomplishments. Yet all the necessary résumé ingredients
are there (a recurring frontal black-and-white photobooth portrait, their name and address all over,
their "classified" bio and awards), to remind us that we are, indeed, looking at two designers, well
versed in typography, excellent in copywriting, and mastering the secrets of the trade. Only they've
wrapped their talent into caustic humor, and boy! does it work. While deconstructing the genre
of self-promotion into a self-critical process, karlssonwilker reveals their work philosophy. The
message is whimsical and simple—in and out of the box: it sounds like "1-800-we-exist," we are
here, we are two designers in New York, available for work, come to our Friday night roof parties,
we are the scouts of a community of design-savvy friends. We are fun to work with.

Laetitia Wolff, Founder
Futureflair

147

Some rudimentary designs for a cool clothing company. Somehow, we never finished the job. (129)

SELF - PROMOTION

RANDOM THOUGHTS
PRECISE PROMOTION

TRUST

SPECIAL

KAPITOLA GÖR!

KAPITOLA GÖR!

la Smolarz, Hjalti Karlsson, and Jan Wilker
ke time out for a smoke in the lounge.

Another restaurant, in downtown Philadelphia. They serve drinks with glowing ice cubes. These green menus were a part of our first presentation.

30 TAPAS

$3 each

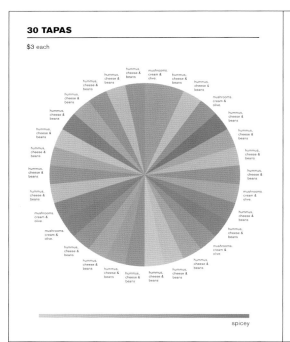

spicey

MENU

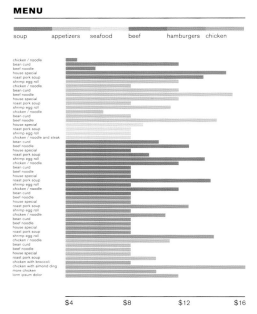

150

50 KINDS OF BEER

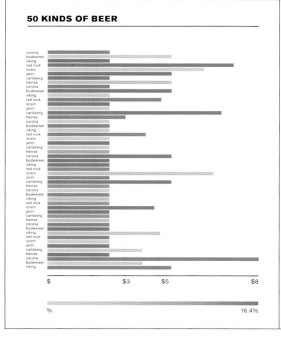

DESSERT

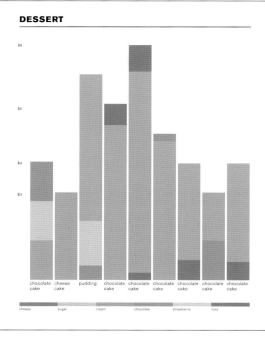

GENTLEMEN

What a pleasure it is for me to share my thoughts about your professional abilities and your unique, creative spirit.

Having found you as the "offspring" of another unique spirit, Stefan Sagmeister, I knew that I would get "out of the box"—correction, "way out of the box"—conceptual approaches to a conventional product base.

To start with I was most impressed with your work ethic, getting the job done on time and on budget. Basics in the world of business, but, believe me, not to be taken for granted. Most special about what I found to be unique about what you do is your sense of humor, your unpredictable twist, and your down-to-earth people sense to graphics, branding, and design.

Usually graphic artists are more concerned with design and less concerned with concept. Your philosophy on the other hand is quite the reverse. Concept dominated design.

I have found that your work provokes, therefore achieves my goal of being noticed. I also find that your work reflects you as human beings and as such you are both wonderful, sensitive, funny, and lovingly freakish. I can't wait to work with you on our next project.

Tony Goldman, Owner/President
Goldman Properties

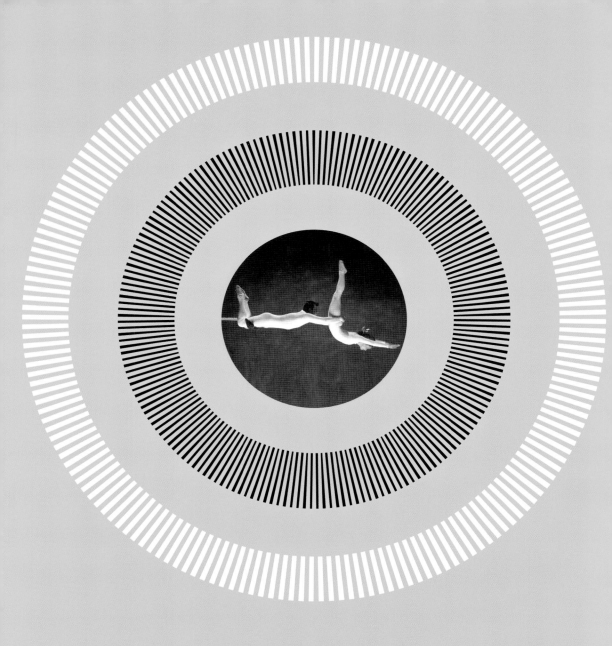

TRUST

a kitchen and bar.

215 (philadelphia) 629 1300. on the corner of 13 & sansom.

25 dollars gift certificate

TRUST

a kitchen and bar. 030

on the corner of 13 & sansom.

215 (philadelphia) 629 1300

TRUST

a kitchen and bar.

lunch and dinner – monday to saturday.
11.30am to 2am.

215 (philadelphia) 629 1300.
on the corner of 13 & sansom.

TRUST

a kitchen and bar. on the corner of 13 & sansom.

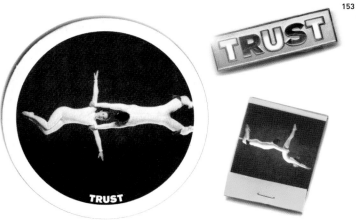

TRUST

TRUST

a kitchen and bar. 215 (philadelphia) 629 1300.

**The final design used all these
cheesy acrobats in their tight leotards.** (135)

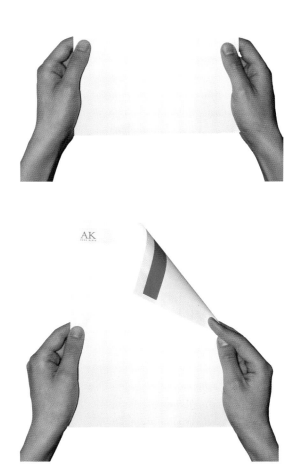

We did the stationery systems for Anne Klein New York and its affiliates. Here: the AK Anne Klein letterhead.

ANNE KLEIN GROUP

ALBERT NIPON

And these are logos we did for the Anne Klein Group and its sublabels.

Pattern design for AK Anne Klein. (140)

OFF THE CHARTS
MEDIA KIT

— PROGRAMMING

— EVENTS

— AUDIENCE

— PRESS

A small portion of two different proposals for a VH1 media kit. The client was disappointed with our work and thought everything was too corporate looking.

Our friends became models for an afternoon photoshoot. (133)

happy holidays

from everyone at karlssonwilker inc.

Happy Holidays from

karlzonwilker

for customer service, call 1 212 929 8064 or visit us at www.karlssonwilker.cor

OF INSPIRATION AND IDIOCY

I didn't get much sleep last night, thanks to my boisterous three-month-old son's decision to make 3 A.M. party time, and now it's 11:20 P.M. and I've just finished another Pale Ale, so this is not coherent, but it might have something to do with music to which Karlsson and Wilker each introduced me, respectively Sigur Ros's CD *Ágaetis Byrjun* and Bela Bartok's "Concerto for Piano no. 3." Both have something to do with nationalism; Bartok's way of making high modern music out of Hungarian peasant tunes and Sigur Ros's new kind of prog rock from Iceland, with Jón Thor Birgisson's falsetto, which we all thought was Icelandic but turns out to be "Hopelandish."

I remember that falsetto floating up Stefan Sagmeister's spiral staircase when Mr. Hjalti worked there a few years ago and just last week I was playing *Svefn-G-Englar* on a long road trip up I-95 and it still sounded sublime with the monotonous road and headlights in the silvery dusk. Bartok's third piano concerto is lyrical and calm, almost resigned; he wrote it for his wife, just before he died in 1945, after he had fled Europe for America, a land he hated, but the war was over and he was contemplating a return to Hungary. He died before the piece was finished and his student, Tibor Serly, completed the last seventeen bars, raising the pleasing idea that this, like most good art, music, and design, is a collaboration.

If nationality, personality, and cultural idiosyncrasies can be applied to the functional traditions of graphic design, in a way that makes cheeky and subversive reference to all that universalist ideology of Modernism, then we have something close to what Karlsson and Wilker do. Their information graphics are applied to arbitrary information, and then further undermined by brazen, self-conscious salesmanship. I noticed the other day that I'd cut up a karlssonwilker holiday card to make into the cover of a mixed tape of obscure holiday songs I'd recorded from WFMU. "Happy holidays from everyone at karlssonwilker inc." below photos of two very serious looking young men in matching ties. You might be fooled into thinking there was an "everyone" other than these two guys, that there was really an "inc." if it weren't for those rock star hair cuts and the fact that they tried to convey numbers and the size of the firm by reprinting the same picture of the same two guys twice. I find that idiotic and inspiring.

Peter Hall, Writer

159

<We participated in the annual battle of company Christmas cards.
These were our contributions. (139)

160

A job for DreamWorks Records.
The project dragged on for about a year and was never produced. (137)

the space behind this window was filled with mean thoughts on april 11th by a stranger.

Our first ever window display. People were freaked out by the date being too similar to September 11th, and they thought the little laser pointers were bombs. In the end every thing was taken down, or it was changed—we are not quite sure. (142)

DECIPHERING THE OFFICE (II):

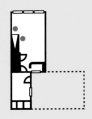

THE IMAC.
64 MB RAM. 6.33 GB HARDDISK.
ON A GOOD DAY 300 MB AVAIL-
ABLE. 350 MHZ. USED FOR INTER-
NET, MAILS, ETC. IT'S OUR OFFICE
MACHINE, WITH FILE MAKER 6.0.
THE ONLY MACHINE WE HAVE
CONNECTED TO THE WEB. CRASH-
ES ALMOST NEVER. WE SHOULD DO
A BACK UP SOON. NO ONE FEELS
RESPONSIBLE FOR THIS ONE. THE
FIRST MACHINE WE BOUGHT. IT
TOOK US 20 MONTHS TO BUY
ADDITIONAL 256 MB RAM.

THE HJALTI-CLONE.
128 MB RAM. 20 GB HARDDISK.
SOMEHOW NEVER MORE THAN 4
GB AVAILABLE. 450 MHZ. MAINLY
USED BY HJALTI. THIS IS THE SEC-
OND MACHINE WE GOT. TOOK US
TOO LONG TO GET AN ADDITIONAL
512 MB RAM. COMPLETELY
CRASHED AFTER FEW WEEKS OF
PURCHASE. HAS ALWAYS BEEN A
LITTLE WEIRD SINCE THEN.

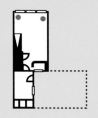

THE JAN-CLONE.
256 MB RAM. 40 GB HARDDISK.
WITH AN AVERAGE OF 6 GB AVAIL-
ABLE. 533 MHZ. MAINLY USED BY
JAN. IT'S THE THIRD MACHINE WE
GOT. AND, AGAIN, IT TOOK US TOO
LONG TO GET AN ADDITIONAL 512
MB RAM. CRASHES SOMETIMES
AND NO ONE KNOWS WHY. EVERY
ONCE IN A WHILE JAN GETS HIM
AN APPOINTMENT WITH THE
DOCTOR.

163

THE TRUE MAC.
96 MB RAM. 4 GB HARDDISK.
RIGHT NOW 800 MB AVAILABLE.
233 MHZ. MAINLY USED BY OUR
INTERNS. THE SCANNER IS
HOOKED UP TO THIS ONE. THE
COMPUTER WAS A MOVING-IN GIFT
FROM STEFAN, THE MONITOR IS
HJALTI'S OLD ONE (THE IMAGE
SHOWS THE WRONG KEYBOARD
AND MOUSE). HE NEVER REALLY
CRASHES.

164

This project kept us busy all summer long.
The CD was shrinkwrapped in 3-color printed plastic.
All the scribbles, scratches, and type were done on the computer.

A selection of things we did. Everyone was happy, especially us.
We loved working on this project. (144)

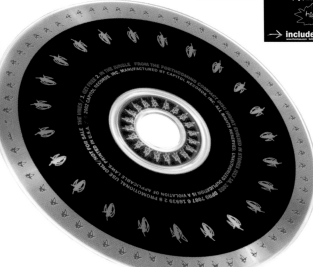

HATTLER MALLBERRY MOON IN STORES NOW

For this Hattler release we had our photographer friend take some action shots of Mr. Hattler himself. In the beginning we didn't really know what for. (211)

HATTLER
MALLBERRY MOON

HATTLER
MALLBERRY MOON

01 MISS AMERICA 4:34
02 TO BED 4:08
03 MALLBERRY MOON 5:03
04 NOT WHAT YOU THINK 4:51
05 GODDESS OF LOVE 3:49
06 SERIOUS 5:19
07 DELHI BLUES 5:12
08 SILENT ADVICE 3:03
09 HERO 4:37
10 NO FUN 7:38
11 NOT THE ONE 3:36
12 NACHTSTROM 7:18

This is the first book project we did in our studio. The die-cut leftovers were used as the invitations and coasters for the book-launch party.

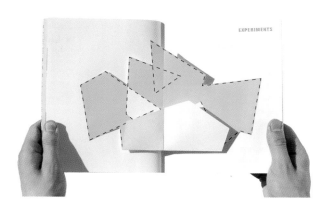

EXPERIMENTS

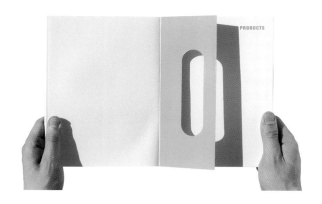

PRODUCTS

ENVIRONMENTS

BOOKLAMP!

EASY TO BUILD!

①

DON'T LET THIS BOOK GET LOST IN YOUR BOOKSHELF!

②

③ BUY: LIGHTBULB, 60 W, MATT SOCKET, SILVER, MATT ELECTRIC CABLE, WHITE

④ ASSEMBLE LAMP

⑤ ENJOY!

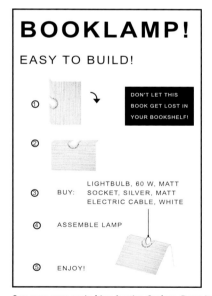

One very very early idea for the *Curious Boym* book. The center spread was foil paper. (138)

MEN SEEKING

I was doing two things at the same time: thinking what to write for the new karlssonwilker book and idly leafing through the personals of *Time Out* magazine (I have no idea why). Eventually, this completely fictional personal ad started to take shape.

OCCUPATION: Graphic designers
AGE: Looking too young and too good to be running a design office
CELEBRITIES THEY RESEMBLE MOST:
Jan: David Byrne
Hjalti: Maybe, John Wayne when he was young
IN THEIR OFFICE YOU'LL FIND:
Samples of CDs and their covers-to-be of every imaginable design
A big TV loaded with video games
Suits on a hanger—always ready for that client meeting
Cold beer in refrigerator—for different, downtown kind of clients
Conference area that looks and feels like a lounge in a nice bar
FAVORITE WORD: Somehow
BIGGEST PROFESSIONAL PROBLEM: One of the two always seems to be in Europe
WHY YOU SHOULD WANT TO KNOW THEM:
Because they have fun doing their work, even when it's for a nominal fee, and they somehow pass this fun on to their clients.
Because even though they may look goofy, they surprise their clients by delivering the job in a professional manner, on time, and without any grief or attitude.
Because they send out funny, weird promotional materials.
Because their office is near all subway stops.
Because they throw a party every three weeks and invite everyone.
WHO THEY ARE LOOKING FOR:
"People who give us work, and who become our friends in the process."

I hope this ad is answered many times over. Chances are, a blind date with these guys will turn into a long-term relationship, as I was fortunate to learn in my personal experience.

Constantin Boym, Founder
Boym and Partners

176

A small logo job for a friend. And this is what it looks like big. (210)

book III

UShdFkMr

introducing our new mascot:

TINY STORIES (11):
the truth is, i never meant to hurt or scare anyone. i am a very
stable person, ask anyone. i don't know what happened that day
and if there was any way that i could take it back i would. i am very
sorry and i would like to apologize to everyone who was affected
and also would like to extend that apology to their families. next
time i begin to feel like i have a very original practical joke i will
definitely consult with the authorities about it's legality before doing
anything about it.

the square:

with
great power comes
great response.

the girl who can't dance says the band can't play.

second left, then
straight ahead.

lying is everybody's everyday fun!

i love you.

lying is everybody's everyday fun!

i didn't know she
was a minor.

lying is everybody's everyday fun!

spongebob

Hjalti and Jan, wearing their big plastic hats:

THIS IS NEW! THE UNBEATABLE CUSTOMER SERVICE:

ALCOHOL IS NOT A SOLUTION. NEVER.

JUST JOKING. IT'S A GREAT STRESS RELIEVER AND IT TASTES GREAT. IT'S CHEAPER THAN FRESH SQUEEZED FRUIT JUICE AND YOU FEEL MORE IN CHARGE. IT TURNS YOU INTO THE COOL GUY THAT YOU ALWAYS WANTED TO BE. THEREFORE IT CAN'T BE THAT BAD. IT'S MORE OF A LIFESTYLE, LIKE SMOKING OR BEING A BAD ASS MOFO. ONE BIG PREJUDICE ABOUT ALCOHOL: IT'S FOR PEOPLE WHO LACK SELF-ESTEEM! HA! THE TRUTH IS THAT IT'S A GREAT EXCUSE FOR BEING RUDE, NOT YOURSELF, NOT ABLE TO STEER YOUR CAR, NOT KNOWING WHAT YOU'RE DOING AND VERY IMPORTANT, FOR MURDER. FFFFFT.

this is you: $\dfrac{1}{6\ 000\ 000\ 000}$

MADE IN AMERICA

BY EUROPEANS.

TINY STORIES (12):

yesterday i ate at a new restaurant. i had heard that the clientele were a cut above the rest. like me. i was surprised to discover that the elite are every bit as tangible as the rest. the food was good, and the preperation impeccable. sometimes when i close my eyes i see lights and i can imagine myself as one great branch on the tree of life. when i open them again all i see is lobster bisque. these twerps here wouldn't know a good lobster bisque from a hole in the head.

some of the most important numbers in use:

II V VII
X XII M

←this design took us 8 (eight) seconds!

freeze } **capture**

go }

Behind the Scenes (4):

Meeting with your parents:

parents: so what did you do lately? still drawing?

designer: ah, yes, sort of...

parents: more potatoes?

THIS IS NEW! THE UNBEA

WHAT WE NEE

(LET'S CALL IT LINGO FOR NOW) LINGO IS YO
RESIDENT OF YOUR COUNTRY AND YOU BETT
MATTER IF IT SNOWS OR RAINS. AND BECA
FRIENDS WITH GOD HIMSELF AND SEX; OH
PLACES AS LINGO.

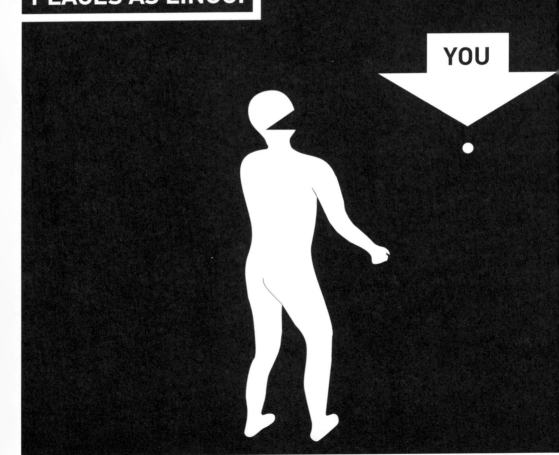

YOU

LE CUSTOMER SERVICE:

IS LANGUAGE

RIEND, MAYBE YOUR BEST FRIEND. IT IS A
ESPECT IT. EVERYDAY IT IS WITH YOU, NO
IT IS ALWAYS AROUND YOU, IT IS GOOD
THESE TWO GUYS HANG AROUND SAME

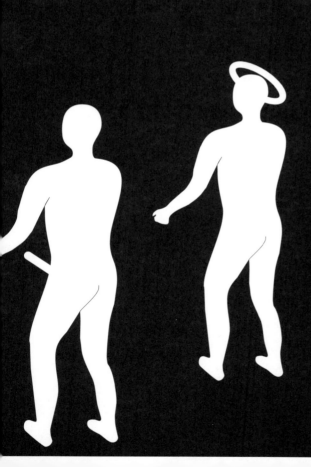

TINY STORIES (13):

i'd been living in the desert with my mom for about a year before i even began to miss the civilized world. we had got into a fight and hadn't really been talking for a few weeks. also, water was becoming harder and harder to find. i told her that i was ready to leave and she just laughed. where are you going to go, she said, there is no civilization anymore. and even if there was, what would you do there. i opened the tent door and stared at the endless horizon of sand. does it end, i thought, ever.

WAR

WAR

design is
now officially
declared
a hobby.

designer's nightmare (1)

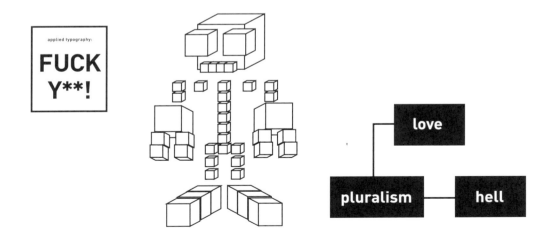

applied typography:

FUCK
Y**!

love

pluralism — hell

people see

designer's nightmare (2)

social and environmental issues become important

designer's nightmare (3)

dear eminem, we really like your music, but look what you do to our children. they all get bad grades...

My name is Eric.

falling in love with an artist

designer's nightmare (4)

power outage

designer's nightmare (5)

responsibility for content

designer's nightmare (6)

complete the following sentence:

Little Johnny will _____ most of his classmates and teachers at school tomorrow.

THIS IS NEW! THE UNBEATABLE CUSTOMER SERVICE:

HAPPY HAPPY IMPLANTS FOR ALL OF US

LET'S GO CRAZY WITH OUR BODIES. THEY'RE OURS. ANYWAY, YOU SHOULD GET A THIRD KNEE. NOW.

TINY STORIES (15):

one day i am going to fight like my old man. he killed a lot of people and that made him tough. i know that when we go out he is always aware of where the exits are and who is around him. once the waiter popped out of nowhere and my dad had him on the floor before you even knew what had happened. i tried to do the same thing to some kid at school, but i got my ass beat. when i told my dad he just shook his head and apologized for being such a bad influence. don't worry dad, i said, that sucker had it coming.

REOLA

What I have to say may sound unspectacular and may not even be striking enough for a comment in a printed book. The reason for this is that our collaboration has a naive and infantile character. Our agreements feel like the ones that children make while playing. Nonetheless, the result is so successful and satisfying....But how exactly do we get there?

I would like to shed some light on our relationship, but I can't really explain our interaction. If I did, no one would ever believe it anyway. In fact, it might even be detrimental for the business. What matters is that I trust them completely. I even use and publish their work sight unseen.

Hellmut Hattler, Musician

193

This is the only project in the book that was not done within, or after, the first two years.
It was designed by Jan two months before we opened up the studio, and somehow left its mark on us. (24)

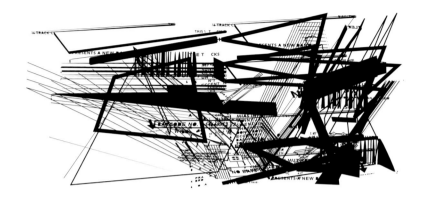

For these two remix CDs we brought back the old files of the main CD (previous page) and used them as the starting point.

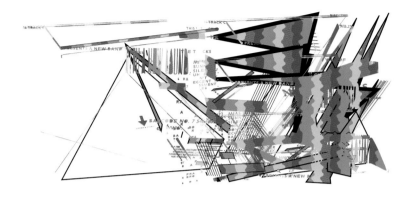

SUNSHINE AND RAINBOWS AND CUTE LITTLE PUPPY DOGS

Karlssonwilker inc. is not a design firm, though you wouldn't know it by flipping through this book or checking out the website or reading about their numerous accomplishments in magazines or what have you. Not that you would think anything was amiss by walking into the office. On the contrary, they've got quite a setup. But just try to use one of those computers...I dare you, just try. Your finger would punch right through the cardboard. Even the X-acto blades are fake. The phones work, though. Yeah, they never stop ringing. Clients? You bet. But I'll be damned if they even know what a graphic design studio is. Forget about it. Those space cases are only interested in one thing. And that one thing is the real foundation upon which the kwinc empire is built.

When I started here, I was carrying around a second-rate design portfolio and struggling to pay my rent. Now I'm wearing Armani suits and dating thousand-dollar-a-night hookers. So much for college, huh? Yeah, well, without the institutional backing I never would have got past security. They figured that if you had an artistic background then you could figure out creative solutions to complex problems. Like, how do you pack a suitcase so customs doesn't get antsy? Or, what is the best way to stop a rival cartel from moving in on your territory? Or, how do you ferret out a mole without letting on that you are on to him? That sort of thing.

But to be honest, my talents lie more on the brute side of things. You know, maybe a client gets the idea that something in the shipment needs to be changed. Maybe they start thinking, "Hey, anybody can do this, why do I gotta pay you so much?" You know, the usual client garbage. Well, in that case, maybe they get a little visit. And maybe the next day the office gets a nice fruit basket apology. Or maybe we just don't hear from them again. And maybe nobody else does either.

So anyway, they call Jan "The Swatch" and Hjalti goes by "Mr. Photoshop." They don't really like it if you use their first names. Especially on the phone. Not that the cops bother us. A monthly shipment of getthehelloffourbackstax keeps them quiet. But with the feds it ain't so easy. They've got no respect for nothing, let alone for honest hardworking businessmen. But I digress. I'm supposed to say something nice about the bosses and that ain't hard to do.

Look, The Swatch and Mr. PhotoShop took me in when I didn't have anything. I had been in and out of prison so many times I pretty much just figured that was where I was going to stay. I mean, I'm not reformed or nothing. I've still got an anger management problem like you wouldn't believe. And if the order comes in, you better hope that you are halfway between here and wherever you are going with your foot on the pedal and a pee-jug between your knees. But their operation lends a touch of class and legitimacy to my "delinquency." I mean, before I worked here everyone just called me a tool. Now I'm known as "The Toolbar." So I gotta bash in a head every now and again. Who doesn't? And besides, now I get respect when I do.

David Lisznia, Designer

The original tape of the **SPOKEN PORTFOLIO**®.

A nicer looking the **SPOKEN PORTFOLIO**®-Cassette could be ordered via phone or by email. A short excerpt should still be on our website. Paul Sahre's sharp observations and his smooth voice made this tape a hit in senior homes.

read what we do! _ _ read what we do! _ _ read what we do! _ _ read what we do!

proudly presenting: the WRITTEN PORTFOLIO®

[The following are excerpts from our WRITTEN PORTFOLIO®. The WRITTEN PORTFOLIO® is the written version
of the SPOKEN PORTFOLIO®. The SPOKEN PORTFOLIO® was originally recorded live on 9/13/02 during a spontaneous
description session at our offices with Mr. PAUL SAHRE featuring his very own voice.]

SEE THROUGH
PAUL'S EYES!

SO LEAN BACK, READ SLOWLY AND WATCH THE IMAGES COME AND GO:

"...it's a jewel case, wrapped in plastic – it's black. and it has 4 images, abstract images, which are (red) scratches, in abstract sha...
possibly (heads)..."–"...there is handwritten typography, which is rendered in a logotype style, but roughly, loosely, that spells out ...
name in the right hand side, underneath two of the scratches..."–"...the back cover is also black..."–"...in the upper left hand corner is a s...
songs, again set in upper and lower case franklin gothic bold, knocked out to white, with red scratches through each of the songs..."–"...
only other thing on the back cover are two logos...in the lower right hand corner...also are scratched out with a red line..."

from: DESIGN FOR A NEW BAND: THE VINES (here: the main cd packaging)
client: capitol records, 2002

"...this book is approximately 9 inches tall by 6 inches wide–and it is approximately an inch thick. it has an orange cover with a die-cut circ...
in the center, revealing part of a chair, that has a raised black leather back to it, with four buttons in the middle..."–"...title...is set centered...
and it's rather large on the cover...appears black against the orange background of the cover...the entire chair revealed...also two figures are
"...when we open the front cover, the die-cut then reveals the entire scene...the spine is of a different material..."–"...
revealed...one...who is crouching off to the right hand side..."

from: BOOK DESIGN: CURIOUS BOYM (a book on boym's 15 years of product design)
client: princeton architectural press, 2002

"...a piece of paper, an 8.5 by 11 sheet of paper, that has the ak anne klein logo on the upper left hand corner, set in a serif font–which might
be a version of garamond..."–"...the logo consists of a large letter a and a large letter k..."–"...this is all in a red color..."–"...logo exists within
a light–which looks to be a 10% screen of the red–bar, which runs across the entire width of the letterhead, but it's printed 100% red on the
paper over...i realized that the light pink screen...is not actually printed on the front of the letterhead, but it's printed 100% red on the
back...so, the effect of the 10% is provided by show-through from this 100% red printed on the back...there is nothing else but this red bar on
the back of this letterhead..."

from: STATIONERY SYSTEMS for all ANNE KLEIN GROUP affiliates (here: ak anne klein letterhead)
client: anne klein group, 2002

"...this is a lamp..."–"...cone-shaped shade..."–"...simple structure to it..."–"...a singular tube of gold metallic material/cylinder, it's quite
thin..."–"...there is a plastic dog at the top of this lamp, head first into the top of the shade..."–"...could be a jack russell terrier–that's gonna
be my guess..."

from: DOGLAMP (a lamp for a good cause)
client: world studio foundation, 2001

"...looks like a bank...from the distance..."–"...the entrance...the two words trust appear on either side of a corner of this overhang..."–"...extra
bold..."–"...an indication, that these two areas of typography would light up at night..."–"...this...has been applied to other pieces that relate to
the restaurant..."–"...t, u and t are die-cut..."–"...gold pin...t, u and t are die-cut out of the metal..."–"...the woman is hanging
030..."–"...two gymnasts dressed in white leotards..."–"...reaching down...knees slightly bent...facing us..."–"...with their arms clasped..."–"...coming from
horizontally..."–"...light gothic...all centered..."–"...black and white images...in various poses..."–"...with their arms clasped...a warm grey, a mustard, navy blue and a light
aqua..."–"...now..."–"...hm..."   the color palette is a muted combination of rust, a warm grey, a mustard, navy blue and a light
the left and right instead from the top..."–"...the color palette is a muted combination of rust, a warm grey, a mustard, navy blue and a light

from: TRUST (concept, naming and design for a restaurant in philadelphia)
client: goldman properties, 2002

HEAR WHAT WE DO!

also available:
through the eyes of Mr. Paul Sahre & his very own voice:
proudly presenting: the SPOKEN PORTFOLIO®
now at www.karlssonwilker.com or order the audio cassette now!

DECIPHERING THE OFFICE (III):

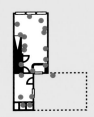

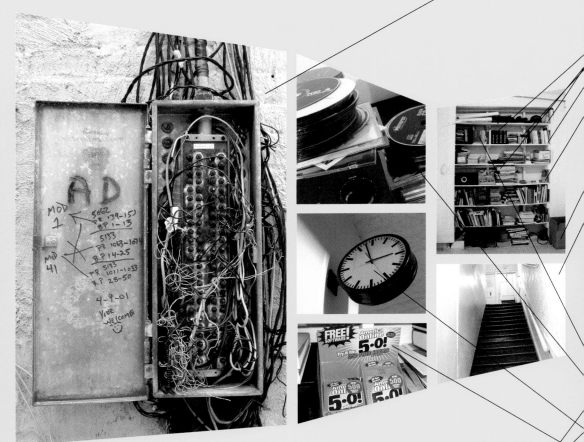

A NON-WORKING FIREPLACE
THE PLAYSTATION WAS UNDER THE TV. IT'S NOW IN JAN'S APARTMENT
THIS LITTLE CABINET HOLDS OUR PAPER SUPPLIES AND EXTRA INK FOR THE PRINTERS
JOB FOLDERS, PHONE BILLS, DESIGNER RESUMES, ETC.
THE PLANTS THAT LOOK NICE
A LITTLE STONE THAT ELLA FOUND
A CLOSE UP OF THE LITTLE HUSKY TOOLBOX. INSIDE ARE OLD PHOTOS AND EXTRA CHECKS

THIS IS OUTSIDE ON OUR ROOFTOP. IT SHOWS HOW OUR BUILDING IS CONNECTED TO THE OUTSIDE
WORLD - PHONE, FAX, INTERNET - EVERYTHING GOES THROUGH HERE.
D&AD SILVER AWARD. HJALTI GOT THIS WHEN HE WORKED WITH STEFAN.
PAPER SAMPLE BOOKS
EXTRA BUSINESS CARDS
THE NEW YORK YELLOW PAGES
OUR 2ND PROMO IS IN THIS BOX
A SMASHING PUMPKINS BOXED SET
EXTRA PAGES FOR OUR DAILY PLANNER
UP THE STAIRS, MAKE A LEFT, AND YOU ARE INSIDE OUR OFFICE
THE OFFICE-CLONE
BROKEN INTERCOM

A PART OF OUR CD COLLECTION
THE CLOCK, TELLING US IT'S TIME FOR LUNCH
WE GOT THIS AT RADIO SHACK
PANTONE BOOKS. WE GOT THEM FOR FREE

THE PRINTER SPREAD:

Let's see if it's true what they say.

box is 100 k

box is 40 c, 40 m,
20 y, and 100 k

0,5% cyan   1% cyan, 1% magenta, 1% yellow

← 0.0001 pt thickness
← 0.001 pt thickness
← 0.1 pt thickness
← 0.2 pt thickness
← 0.5 pt thickness
← 1 pt thickness
← 1.1 pt thickness
← 1.15 pt thickness
← 3 pt thickness
← 15 pt thickness

| 69% | 68% | 67% | 66% | 65% | 64% | 63% | 62% | 61% | 60% | 59% |

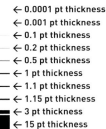

 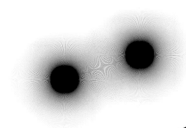

HOW DID THE PRINTER TRIM THE BOOK?
(this line should be aligned with the bottom)

this is 1pt type→ --------

5% yellow

10% yellow

darker?

ORIGINAL

The end of the document was right here

UNSHARPEN
AMOUNT: 17%
RADIUS: 1.3 PIXELS
THRESHOLD: 0 LEVELS

UNSHARPEN
AMOUNT: 190%
RADIUS: 8.5 PIXELS
THRESHOLD: 43 LEVELS

helvetica

hjalti refuses to
see a difference
between these
typefaces.

din

hjalti refuses to
see a difference
between these
typefaces.

trade gothic

hjalti refuses to
see a difference
between these
typefaces.

hello there.
how is it going?

4 pt type in a 100k box

hello there.
how is it going?

4 pt type in a 60c 60m 40y 100k box

The CD package for the Sverrisson/Gudjonsson Duo recording. The Music on this CD is solely inspired by family occasions. We went through both of the musicians' old family albums, then recropped the chosen images. (212)

IT'S BETTER TO HEAR THE RAIN

The first thing I noticed about Hjalti and Jan is how much they dislike design and how homesick they are. Their work is clearly a cry for help.

You can say the same thing about CDs, trapped in their little plastic boxes. But Hjalti and Jan seem to have spent years trying to improve the situation of the CD cover. Looking at it endlessly, thinking we can't just decorate this thing, we have to give it personality. It has to go out there and communicate.

It has been suggested that visual communication is a bit crude compared to sound. Yet our culture has become more and more visual by the minute. Images flashing by to the point that we don't notice them anymore. But the image never seems to be the center of Hjalti and Jan's work. What you see is an organization of ideas that, much like music, has a plot and process. This seems to make the work more of an inner experience than a direct eye stimulus.

Other things they could improve: dance instructions, inner-city planning, names for bands, traffic signs, propaganda, rumors.

Skúli Sverrisson, Musician

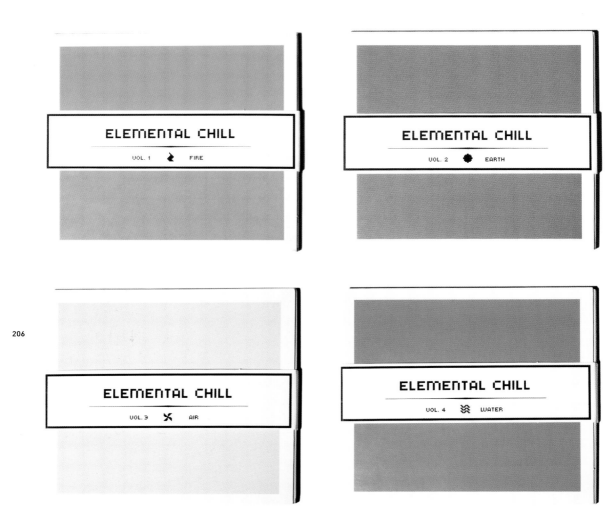

206

Packaging for a four CD compilation, simple colored Digipaks® with bellybands.
The circles on the CD are the barcodes. We got a kick out of it. (212)

IT WAS THE SUMMER OF '69

Oh wait, no it wasn't. Hjalti Karlsson and Jan Wilker arrived on my radar via a newsprint promo they sent to me in 2001. This was the beginning of a great friendship. Through their graphics alone, they communicated their cleverness, their humor, their sly take on life. I liked it. I hired them. The results speak for themselves. Check it out. I count them among my friends. They are my touchstones for wry commentary on the human being, the witty end to a long day. The two people behind karlssonwilker fill my cup and I am greedy...could I possibly have another? And they throw great parties. Word!

Beth Sereni, A&R Manager
Kriztal Entertainment

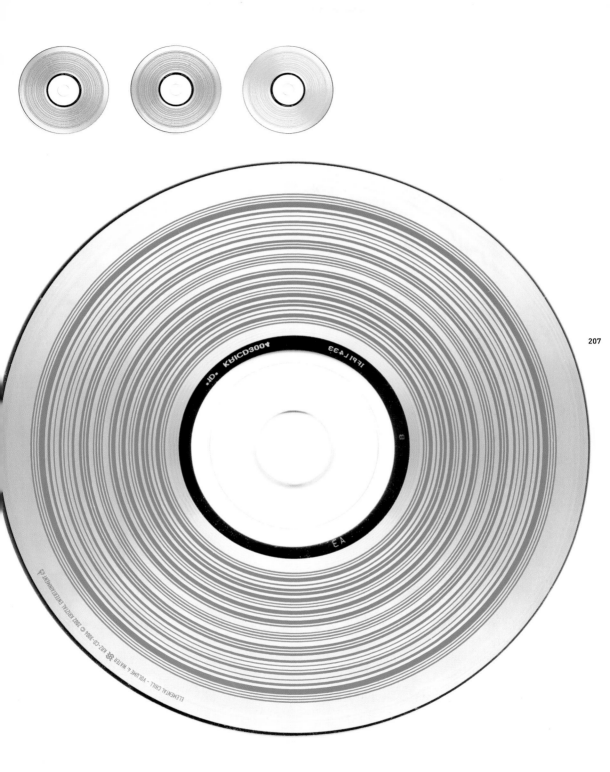

THINGS SHARED WITH KARLSSONWILKER

door	package delivery	digital camera	stories
hallway	sending emails	jim white cd	address
building	receiving emails	lunch	landlord
lounge	sending faxes	books	view
buses	receiving faxes	interns	blinds
loiterers	fedex labels	opinions	air
strange neighbors	air conditioner storage	x-men chocolate	smells
parades	no one will pick up our	beer	music
sid	garbage	beer	headaches
men looking for prosti-	doing too much free work	beer	plumbing
tutes	fucking retroactive taxes	beer	floor paint
dunkin' donuts	(which we still haven't	beer	water company
dunkin' donuts coffee	paid)	beer	messenger company
mice	september 11	stress	dsl (verizon)
frank	plunger	thoughts	parties
primal screams	folding chairs	pantone book (they still	hangovers
introductions to people	hammer	have it)	fines
from iceland	level	the spoken portfolio	publisher
introductions to people	boombox (i still have it)	the leisurama	
from germany	corkscrew	longboard	Paul Sahre,
introductions to people	strathmore paper sample	squash	Graphic Designer and
from upstate new york	book	filemaker	Educator
package pick-up	intercoms	connections	Office of Paul Sahre

Story continued from page 144 Capitol loves the scratches. They use them on everything—bin cards, store banners, tour posters, pins, Website, ads, and the CD's shrink-wrapping—everything but the CD liner itself, arguably the most important component of the design job. Once the shrink-wrapping is removed, the CD takes on a completely different look. It is graced—or disgraced, depending on how you look at it—by a somewhat sophomoric painting of vines by the band's front man, Craig Nicholls.

No one likes the painting—no one but Craig. The designers and the people at Capitol do everything they can to prevent it from appearing anywhere but in Craig's parents' hallway. Three of Capitol's top executives come to karlssonwilker's office to try to prevent the inevitable. Jan covers the office alone, as Hjalti is away in Iceland. The executives arrive on time, then spend the next two hours busying themselves on their phones and text messengers until Craig and his manager show up. Jan shows everyone several schemes for how the CD could look without Craig's painting, and the painter throws a fit. This is not particularly unusual—music executives are practiced in managing such outbursts. But they do not know how to manage this one. It is more than just a tantrum—Craig seems on the point of a breakdown. And with both an MTV interview and a live concert coming up later in the day, they decide to back off. The painting will print.

The executives leave, but Craig stays. He likes it at karlssonwilker. In fact, *he* thinks *Jan* is cool. How exciting it is to have your own office and to work on design all day. He sits next to Jan at his computer that afternoon and half of the next day, making suggestions for the CD design and reveling in all the fun. Jan does not mind the company. He finds Craig charming, for all his quirkiness. Craig is a bit on the edge, and this makes things interesting. At one point, Ella has to walk him across the street to McDonald's because he is too scared by the view outside the office window to make the trip himself. He asks if the four dollars in his pocket is enough to buy a donut downstairs. When he wants to phone a friend, Jan has to dial the number for him. When all these trials are over, they have a design. The CD liner is filled with solid blocks of color taken from the painting, both referencing the erratic artwork and quieting it down a bit. The credit in the liner notes reads, "Designed in one day by Craig Nicholls and Jan Wilker at karlssonwilker inc., NYC."

Highly Evolved is released in July 2002. Soon the Vines appear on the MTV Music Awards and on an MTV concert from the Rock and Roll Hall of Fame. In September, they are on the cover of *Rolling Stone*, and in December, on the cover of *The Face*. The more exposure they get, the better for karlssonwilker. For the first time in a long time, Hjalti and Jan feel that their office is safe.

Design Pimpin'. Bigtime.
The phones are ringing off the hooks at karlssonwilker. It would be such a nice story that, after all Hjalti and Jan's hard work, the Vines bring them their big break, and Coke and Pepsi are now phoning them at all hours. But unfortunately, these are all unwanted calls, the calls of toner salesmen, fire-extinguisher inspectors, and Republican party recruiters. Hjalti and Jan refer these calls to their

209

colleague "Bobby," who just never seems to be around. "I'm sorry, but Bobby handles that, and he's not in right now." "I'm sorry, Bobby will be out on vacation for the next two weeks." A call from Galacy, a Website development company, should have been sent directly to Bobby, but it makes Hjalti curious. Galacy "has seen karlssonwilker's Website" and can "offer it a much better design for only $20." This sounds like too much fun for Bobby, so Hjalti signs up.

A month later, he notices a charge from Galacy on the Verizon bill. He phones the company and insists it remove the charge, as it has done no work. Mr. Galacy insists it has and gives karlssonwilker a password to its site, where Hjalti finds a few lousy templates for Web design. He asks to talk to the company's manager, and the same voice returns to the line, after a slight pause. Finally, Hjalti bursts out, "Who are you? You sound like some guy in his basement in New Jersey!" The line goes dead.

Without Coke or Pepsi on board, karlssonwilker takes what it can get. Sometimes this is not the most prized work, like a May print ad campaign publicizing an upcoming Tom Hanks tribute show. The client is cable giant USA Network, which sounds "bigtime" to Hjalti and Jan, but the job is to tweak an in-house proposal, which includes some less-than-bigtime Herb Ritts photographs of the actor on a tricycle. The network likes karlssonwilker's redesign, but in the end reverts to its in-house scheme.

The office's next client—a New York– and Miami-based law firm that does mediation for photographers, designers, and the like—offers no such visions of grandeur. Its owner wants "something special, something clever" for her business card; she needs to impress creative clients with her own creativity. Jan proposes a straightforward logo on the front and a split logo on the back that when ripped in half can be put together to form the complete logo. This can be a hit at cocktail parties, an interactive and memorable symbol of the mediation that the company performs. The owner is not so sure about the design. Maybe she needs something simpler. Maybe she does not need color on the card. Maybe she needs to change the copy. The client stalls and stalls. First she needs to show it to her friends. Then she is going on vacation and cannot make a decision. Then she might not do anything at all. Finally, she stops returning karlssonwilker's phone calls. And she is smart enough—or at least enough of a lawyer—to have never signed a contract with the designers.

Jan gets a little job from his friend Gabor Salgo, his cofounder in the Sharksucker surfing apparel company. Gabor is a doctor in Munich and has plans to open his own company, Salgo Medical Care, someday. Jan designs a little logo for him, which he loves, so that is all that matters.

Hjalti misses all of these short episodes while he is taking some time off in Iceland. Working alone is a nice change for Jan. Even the best relationships are strained sometimes, and the two men can use a break from each other. Jan finds that he can get a lot done when he is alone. He has no one to mess around with, no one to distract him from his work. And if the work is not done, he has no one to blame but himself. In fact, he is not completely alone—Daniel, the intern, still comes

210

Hjalti and Jan get a call from Beth Sereni in August. It has been a year since they disappointed each other with the DJ Baby Anne project, but now there are no hard feelings. Beth is very professional about karlssonwilker's inability to please her. "These things happen," she says. Her Miami company, Pandisc Records, has a new name—Kriztal Entertainment—and a new focus, "bringing quality music spanning down tempo/chill out/lounge/broken beat/jazz to the US." They are planning a series of four CDs dubbed "Vintage Chill," which they plan to market to retail venues as well as wineries—nothing like a little ambient electronica to go with your Chardonnay. Hjalti and Jan are happy for the offer, happy that they did not burn their bridges with DJ Baby Anne.

They begin work by combining a script font appropriate for wine lovers with flashy colors that say, hey, we are not too stodgy. A belly band mimicking a wine label finishes the piece. But on the day they are to turn the project in, Beth calls with some bad news. Vintage Chill is canceled—the wineries are out. Kriztal is going to repackage the CDs for retail outlets alone and so redefine the "four seasons" theme of the former project to "four elements": earth, fire, water, and air. Hjalti and Jan have two days to submit a new scheme for Elemental Chill.

The good news is that the designers do not feel compelled to keep the "tasteful" serif font from the Vintage Chill package. They instead use a friend's newly drawn Subcaps font, which hints at electronica, along with Din, their much-loved in-house font. Then they pull back on the heavy-handed colors of the cardboard case and use more muted tones to suggest the elements. Color is the only thing on the Digipak except for a small symbol representing an element, which is typically hidden under the belly band containing all the CD's text. The band produces a challenge—if it is removed, the CD's all-important bar code is gone. The designers solve this by printing the bar code on the disc itself, running it around in a circle from edge to edge. Beth is pleased with the design, and Hjalti and Jan are pleased that she has agreed to the expense and opportunity of the Digipak and belly band. Elemental Chill is available now in a music store near you, though not at your local winery.

Björk Doesn't Call.
It is turning out to be a fun summer, both at work and outside of it. When the weather is nice, the partners take a break and sit out on their roof deck, overlooking their many neighbors without access to the sunny spot. Someday soon they will buy a table and deck chairs, maybe even a wading pool. For now they are happy enough to have a table-top hibachi to barbecue burgers—that will surely scare away the smell of donuts. Jan pulls out his tennis racquet from its place in the corner of the office and spends a day or two on a local court. Hjalti grabs the bike that spends most of the year rusting on the roof deck and pedals around Central Park. The summer brings only one day of hardship, when Con Edison accidentally cuts their power line. But even this cannot lower their summer high. They are not able to work without computers and phones and music, and so move their office chairs to the sidewalk and spend the day watching all the action on Sixth Avenue.

They bring their good mood to the work that they do for themselves. The June *Graphis* job starts them on developing all kinds of new fun ideas to represent who they are. They periodically play with these over the course of the summer and then collect them into another mailer. It is time to press for new clients. They call the piece "Welcome to Color," and, of course, print it in black and white. They decide to move from a folded poster to a twelve-page "newspaper." It has been over a year since their first mailer, and they want to show how far they have progressed.

Some of the pages show single enlarged images from the *Graphis* piece. But most are crammed full of new drawings and sayings, all competing for attention. There are elements so bold they are hard to ignore, like the call for panties, and elements so small they are hard to find, like the miniscule type that reads, "…and karim got aroused by the shape he had just created. yes, he changed his little world once again." The process of making each element, even the most intricate process that they know only they will notice, is fun. They get to print some of their failed designs, like the guy with a camera mounted on a backpack from their lost Moth job. Then they use the picture of themselves in suits as a centerfold again, replacing the pencil and heart that were on their lapels with a bomb and a die, and replacing their faces with heads made from three-dimensional type. Their faces move to the back page.

They take the mailer to the printer who did their previous work. To demonstrate their improved station in the design world they upgrade its materials. They hope this is a piece that people will save, collect, and sell for a fortune on eBay in twenty years, so they use better ink and whiter paper and buy the right stamps ahead of time. They send out the first few mailers with their ends protruding from a folded piece of yellow paper, but soon fear this method will get dirty, and so send the rest of the seven hundred in yellow envelopes.

Hjalti and Jan do not release the mailer until they update their Website. One job motivates the other, and they can promote the two simultaneously. They add new projects, their work section so full they need to edit out the weaker or older ones. They put colors on their homepage—a rainbow selection of green to yellow to blue fade in and out behind their boxed logo—then take the colors off, deciding the screen looks better in black and white, then they put them back on again, then take them off. Currently, they are on again. The largest addition to the site is a spoken portfolio®, with commentary by Paul Sahre. His background as an educator and his baritone voice add a depth to their projects. To set this up Hjalti and Jan invite Paul downstairs, seat him in front of a microphone, and feed him projects and corresponding information sheets. Paul critiques all the work extemporaneously in one thirty-minute session:

On the dog lamp: "There is a plastic dog at the top of this lamp, head first into the top of the shade…could be a jack russell terrier—that's going to be my guess…"

On *Curious Boym*: "It has an orange cover with a die-cut circle in the center, revealing part of a chair that has a raised black leather back to it, with four buttons in the middle…"

LEARNING TO FLY

If you've ever followed the career of a superhero for any length of time you know that you eventually get interested in their creation story. You want to know where this person came from, how he became a hero and how she graduated to Super−. You want to hear about Bruce Wayne's salad days, and take a look inside Wonder Woman's high school yearbook. Creation stories are fascinating, because they show our heroes before they climbed the pedestal, when they were more like us. They allow easier access to the fantasy that it could happen to you or me.

This interest in what came before now affects how I look at designers I admire. I see the bulk of their work at shows, in books, or on high-profile assignments—an automatic greatest hits collection. Thus, these artists soon acquire a dazzling sheen of constant inspiration and perfection, which adds to their allure, but doesn't necessarily inspire me in my struggle to grow. Constant success is a lousy roadmap to follow.

So over the years I have taken to collecting the early works of my favorite contemporary designers. The kind of stuff that is now very much missing from their websites and monographs. There is John Warwicker's sleeve for Sting's 1986 *Bring on the Night* live album, or the 1987 Swing Out Sister debut "It's Better to Travel" designed by Me Company. And let's not forget the 1989 album *Big Bang*! by Fuzzbox, a very early export of the Designers Republic. All perfectly fine, attractive pieces, professionally done (and, in the case of DR, already showing small signs of things to come), but in the end...not the artistic clarion calls these people would sound later in their careers.

This, to me, is heartening: my heroes did not spring forth fully formed, radiating genius the minute they got to work. No misunderstood singularities they, who finally got discovered after years of underground brilliance. No. Before their switches got flipped, they worked hard at normal careers, chipping away, getting gigs, doing OK. *Then* their lights came on and they made their big contributions.

So there is hope for you and me, too.

Now Jan and Hjalti are allowing us a glimpse behind their particular curtain: their creation story, documented as it's happening, before the aesthetic skeletons can be carefully stashed in the back of the closet.

This is an interesting dare, because it does demand future greatness.

Right now they're very good designers, Hjalti and Jan. They do smart, entertaining work that makes the world a little safer for all us émigré weirdoes. And for that I am thankful. But I'm counting on them to do something *really big* in a few years. Right now they're just starting to dress up in capes and spandex. I'm waiting for them to take flight.

Then *tellmewhy* will live up to its name. Then we can search this diary of their first two years for the seeds of what was just around the corner.

Stefan G. Bucher, Founder
344 Design

AND THIS IS WHAT HAPPENED AFTER THE FIRST 24 MONTHS, UNTIL THE FINAL FILES OF THIS BOOK WENT TO ASIA TO BE PRINTED:

  We design a book, *A Year in the Life of Andy Warhol,* of never-before-published photographs by David McCabe, taken from 1964 to 1965. It will be published in the fall of 2003. The book starts out with a white background, which gets gradually darker and darker, until it is black. The client is happy. We are happy.

A guy from Issey Miyake calls for our portfolio. We would love to work with him on pretty much anything. Nothing has happened yet.

Hjalti goes more frequently to the gym.

We buy a LaCie external hard drive. It can hold up to 120 GB and is named the Office-Clone.

We work with Rick Albert of Swoop, Inc. on some redesigns for Oscar de la Renta's Pink label and on logos for Calvin Klein.

 We work with the Boyms on an exhibition design, *A Day in the Life of Africa,* at Grand Central Station. They design the exhibition, we lay out the whole show.

We are not as stressed out about everything as before.

A London partner of Pentagram calls and wants to know if we are interested in contributing our work to a book about one hundred young international designers. We are, so we send over some samples. The book will be published in the fall of 2003.

We put a little light above our bar.

We design a new CD package for Verbena. David Lisznia takes all the photos (he and Jan go down to Birmingham for a three-day shoot). The model, Sarah Amsterdam, is thirteen. She is David's little sister.

We meet with Richard Wilde from SVA to talk about teaching, and it looks like we will in the fall of 2003. He invites us to a nice lunch.

We get an email from the senior vice president of Puma. We would really like to work with them on the right project. Hjalti owns a pair of their shoes.

Hjalti moves back into his apartment with Vera. He throws out his old crappy chair and buys a new nice, ultralong sofa. His name is Leif.

Jan and Ella get their own place in funky Williamsburg.

Warner Brothers calls. We will design a CD for Triumph The Insult Comic Dog.

Our friend Rick brings in a job for Gerber...

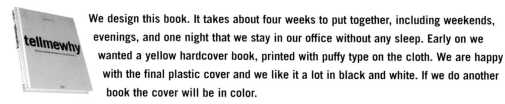

We design this book. It takes about four weeks to put together, including weekends, evenings, and one night that we stay in our office without any sleep. Early on we wanted a yellow hardcover book, printed with puffy type on the cloth. We are happy with the final plastic cover and we like it a lot in black and white. If we do another book the cover will be in color.

And we go through our files and database and put the numbers into some statistics.
A lot of discoveries and surprises for us.

That's all we can think of.
For comments, questions, thoughts, or whatever else, email us
at tellmewhy@karlssonwilker.com.
And you can visit us anytime at www.karlssonwilker.com.

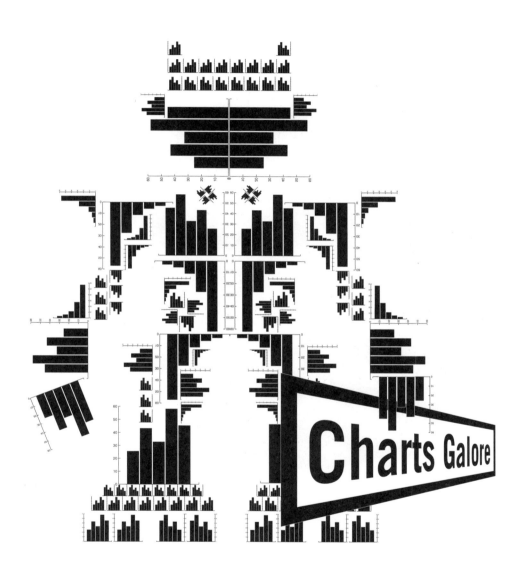

WHAT KIND OF PROJECTS DID WE WORK ON?

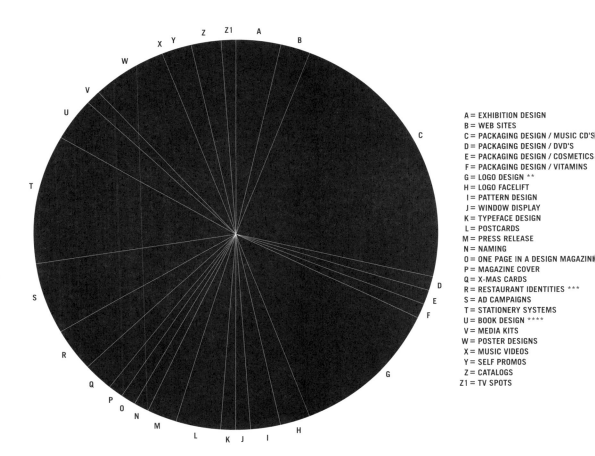

A = EXHIBITION DESIGN
B = WEB SITES
C = PACKAGING DESIGN / MUSIC CD'S*
D = PACKAGING DESIGN / DVD'S
E = PACKAGING DESIGN / COSMETICS
F = PACKAGING DESIGN / VITAMINS
G = LOGO DESIGN **
H = LOGO FACELIFT
I = PATTERN DESIGN
J = WINDOW DISPLAY
K = TYPEFACE DESIGN
L = POSTCARDS
M = PRESS RELEASE
N = NAMING
O = ONE PAGE IN A DESIGN MAGAZINE
P = MAGAZINE COVER
Q = X-MAS CARDS
R = RESTAURANT IDENTITIES ***
S = AD CAMPAIGNS
T = STATIONERY SYSTEMS
U = BOOK DESIGN ****
V = MEDIA KITS
W = POSTER DESIGNS
X = MUSIC VIDEOS
Y = SELF PROMOS
Z = CATALOGS
Z1 = TV SPOTS

* INCLUDES: SINGLES, ADVANCE CD'S, ETC.
** FREESTANDING LOGOS
*** INCLUDES LOGO DESIGNS, POSTCARDS,
    T-SHIRTS, MENUS, ETC.
**** INCLUDING THIS ONE

WHERE DID OUR MONEY GO?

(DAILY AVERAGE OF 2.5 PEOPLE IN THE OFFICE; FIRST 24 MONTHS)

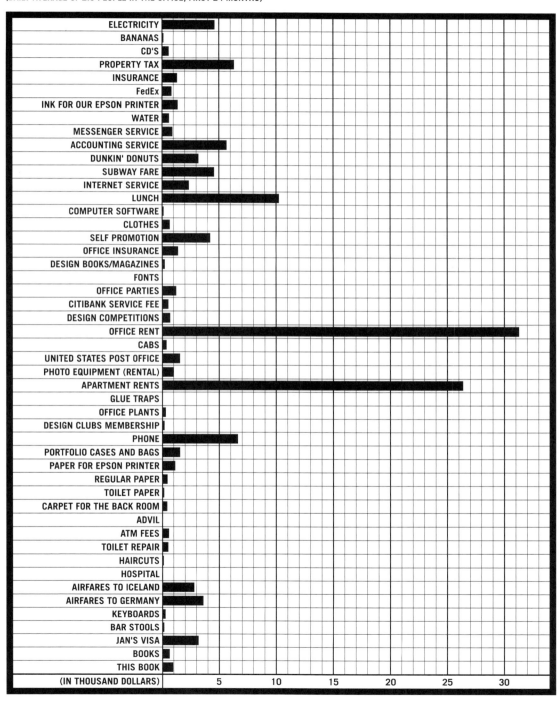

| | 5 | 10 | 15 | 20 | 25 | 30 |

ELECTRICITY
BANANAS
CD'S
PROPERTY TAX
INSURANCE
FedEx
INK FOR OUR EPSON PRINTER
WATER
MESSENGER SERVICE
ACCOUNTING SERVICE
DUNKIN' DONUTS
SUBWAY FARE
INTERNET SERVICE
LUNCH
COMPUTER SOFTWARE
CLOTHES
SELF PROMOTION
OFFICE INSURANCE
DESIGN BOOKS/MAGAZINES
FONTS
OFFICE PARTIES
CITIBANK SERVICE FEE
DESIGN COMPETITIONS
OFFICE RENT
CABS
UNITED STATES POST OFFICE
PHOTO EQUIPMENT (RENTAL)
APARTMENT RENTS
GLUE TRAPS
OFFICE PLANTS
DESIGN CLUBS MEMBERSHIP
PHONE
PORTFOLIO CASES AND BAGS
PAPER FOR EPSON PRINTER
REGULAR PAPER
TOILET PAPER
CARPET FOR THE BACK ROOM
ADVIL
ATM FEES
TOILET REPAIR
HAIRCUTS
HOSPITAL
AIRFARES TO ICELAND
AIRFARES TO GERMANY
KEYBOARDS
BAR STOOLS
JAN'S VISA
BOOKS
THIS BOOK

(IN THOUSAND DOLLARS)

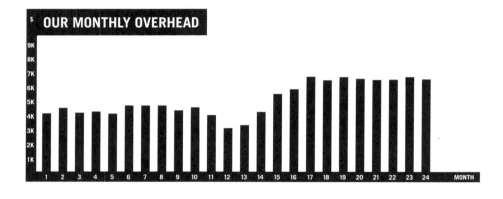

UNNECESSARY

PRODUCTIVE

LEGITIMATE

THINGS WE NEEDED TO IMPROVE ON:

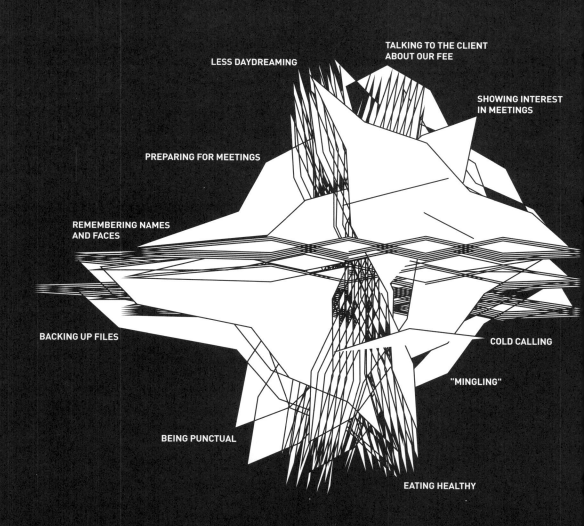

LESS DAYDREAMING

TALKING TO THE CLIENT
ABOUT OUR FEE

SHOWING INTEREST
IN MEETINGS

PREPARING FOR MEETINGS

REMEMBERING NAMES
AND FACES

BACKING UP FILES

COLD CALLING

"MINGLING"

BEING PUNCTUAL

EATING HEALTHY

GOOD **BAD**

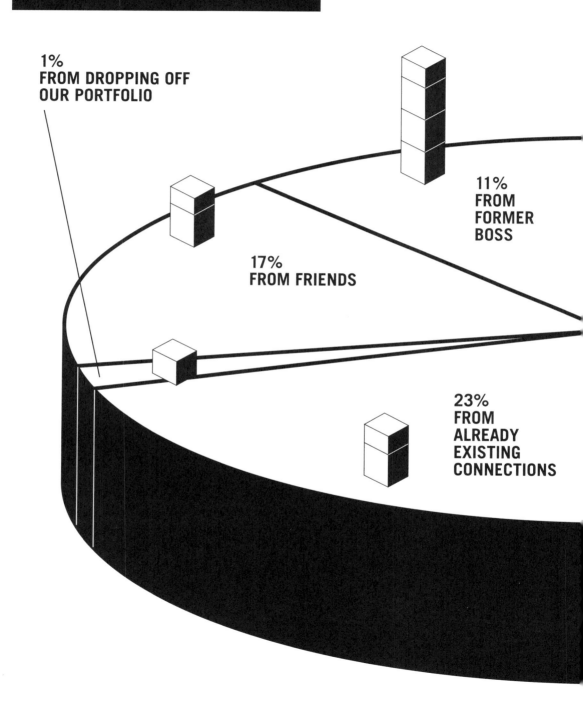

HOW DID WE GET PROJECTS
AND HOW MUCH DID THEY PAY

1%
FROM DROPPING OFF
OUR PORTFOLIO

11%
FROM
FORMER
BOSS

17%
FROM FRIENDS

23%
FROM
ALREADY
EXISTING
CONNECTIONS

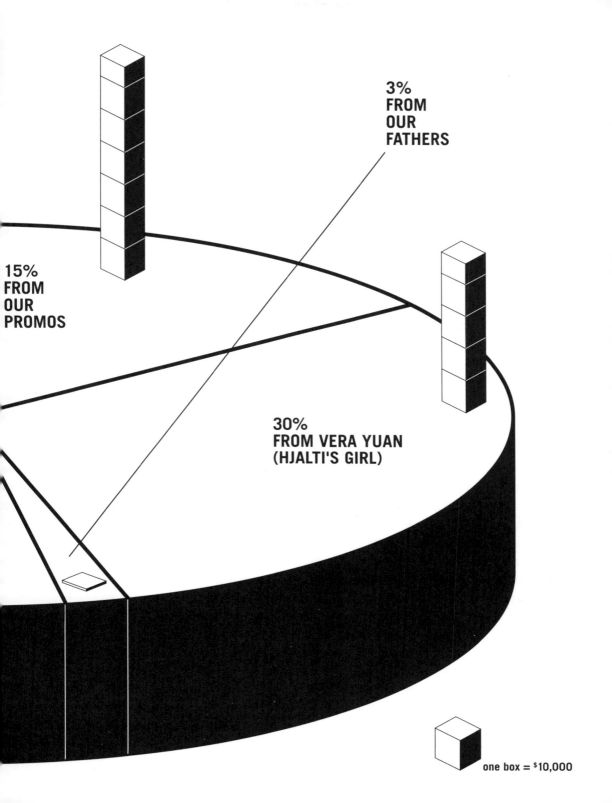

3%
FROM
OUR
FATHERS

15%
FROM
OUR
PROMOS

30%
FROM VERA YUAN
(HJALTI'S GIRL)

one box = $10,000

THE OFFICE IN LISTINGS

MOST PLAYED CDs	FAVORITE CLIENTS	LEAST FAVORITE PROJECTS	FAVORITE GAMES IN THE OFFICE	DAYS CALLED IN SICK
Radiohead – Kid A	Hattler	Icelandic Embassy invite	Grand Theft Auto	Hjalti: 1
Putte and Edgar – Betaversion	Constantin Boym	New York Pops	Pac Man	Jan: 2
Pu – Seepferdchenalbum	Tony Goldman	36 Crazyfists	Dig Dug	Interns: 9
Radiohead – Amnesiac	Capitol Records	Pee Cone	Coin Throwing	Clients: 1
Gay Dad – Leisure Noise	PAP	Piaffe	Armwrestling	Cleaning lady: 0
MOST POPULAR BREAKFAST	**NICE VISITORS TO OUR WEBSITE**	**MOST IMPORTANT IN THE OFFICE**	**WORST PRESENTATIONS**	**SOME BOOKS WE READ**
Donuts from Dunkin' Donuts	Disney	Old files burned on CDs	D.A.P.	LTI
Egg and ham sandwich	Chanel USA	Office Database	Ultra Records	Fast Food Nation
Hot and Crusty roll	Rockstar Games	Hjalti-clone	Nickelodeon	The Power of Now
Chicken noodle soup	Japanese Government	Jan-clone	Vitra	Word Freak
Large Coffee	FBI	Stereo	Vh1	The Art of Mackin'
MOST POPULAR LUNCH	**FUN PROJECTS**	**SMALLEST JOBS**	**OUR INTERNS**	**OUR INTERNS (Cont.)**
Chinatown Take Out	The Vines	*Soho Rep Window display, $60	Allejandra Santos	Sabina Hahn
KFC	Trust Restaurant	Party invite for Boym book, $85	Miriam Wilker	Daniel Pepice
Subway	El Diner	Hollenbeck poster, $90	Daniella Schachter	–
Mondello Family Pizza	Curious Boym	Promo for Boym, $99.99	Jean Lee	–
The Corner Deli	Doglamp	GSM press sheets, $200	Cedric Suming	–
IMPORTANT TELEPHONE NUMBERS	**FASTEST PAID INVOICES**	**SLOWEST PAID INVOICES**	**DREAM CLIENTS**	**BEST FILE NAMES**
(212) 337 1460	2.5 weeks	26 weeks	Jive Records	Untitled art 1
(212) 890 2700	3 weeks	22 weeks	Karl Lagerfeld	Untitled art 2
*69	4 weeks	21 weeks	Robbie Williams	Untitled art 3
FIND A GUN, CALL 911	5.5 weeks	18 weeks	Tourist Board of Hawaii	Untitled art 4
1-800-NO-COPIES	6 weeks	16 weeks	Steven Spielberg	***
MOST USED WORDS: OFFICE	**MOST USED WORDS: INTERNS**	**BIGGEST WORRIES**	**JAN'S FAVORITES**	**HJALTI'S FAVORITES**
Shit	But	Money	Tekken	DVD player
Hungry	Why	Getting new jobs	Beach	Pac Man
Yes	karlssonwilker inc.	Hairline	Books	Icelandic hot dogs
No	Yes	Rapid Belly Growth	Water	Sigur Ros
Hi	Sure	Carpal Tunnel Syndrome	Sponge Bob	Mom & Dad
FAVORITE LUNCH DRINKS	**MOST USED WORDS: CLIENTS**	**SHITTY THINGS IN THE MAIL BOX**	**SOME PEOPLE**	**FAVORITE COLORS**
Coke	Hello	Bills	Arthur Schnitzler	black
Water	What	Printers' promos	Vincent Gallo	white
Coffee	When	Photography promos	Victor Klemperer	off yellow
Fresca	Why	Illustrators' postcards	Rutger Hauer	dark blue
Iced tea	How	Dell Computer Catalogs	Madonna	flashy green

*This is the only invoice that never got paid.

NUMBER OF WEEKENDS NO ONE STOPPED BY THE OFFICE:

7

PHONE CALLS ASKING US TO SWITCH OUR PHONE SERVICE:

53

NUMBER OF PAUL'S REQUESTS TO LOWER THE MUSIC:

18

THE MOVEMENT OF OUR RECEEDING HAIRLINE OVER THE PAST TWO YEARS AND IN THE FUTURE (ABSTRACT RENDERING):

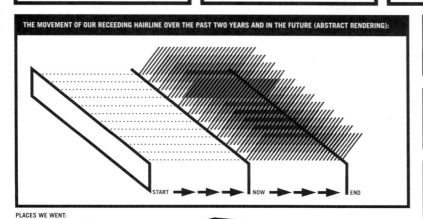

START → → → NOW → → → END

AMOUNT OF DAYS JAN AND HJALTI DIDN'T SEE OR TALK TO EACH OTHER:

42

FEW THINGS WE WEREN'T PREPARED FOR:

TAXES
HARDWARE PROBLEMS
THE FACT THAT MOST CLIENTS DON'T PAY
    WITHIN A MONTH

FEW GREAT THINGS WE GOT IN THE BEGINNING WITHOUT KNOWING THEY WERE GREAT:

GOOD CHAIRS
GOOD CEILING LIGHTS
WATER COOLER
FILEMAKER 6.0 (FOR OUR DATABASE)

PLACES WE WENT:

THE CHART OF YOU:

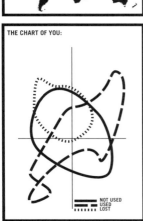

NOT USED
USED
LOST

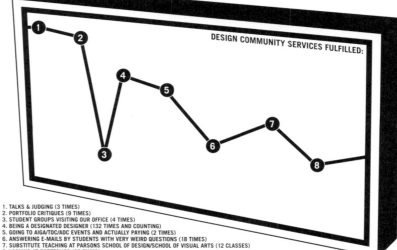

DESIGN COMMUNITY SERVICES FULFILLED:

1. TALKS & JUDGING (3 TIMES)
2. PORTFOLIO CRITIQUES (9 TIMES)
3. STUDENT GROUPS VISITING OUR OFFICE (4 TIMES)
4. BEING A DESIGNATED DESIGNER (132 TIMES AND COUNTING)
5. GOING TO AIGA/TDC/ADC EVENTS AND ACTUALLY PAYING (2 TIMES)
6. ANSWERING E-MAILS BY STUDENTS WITH VERY WEIRD QUESTIONS (18 TIMES)
7. SUBSTITUTE TEACHING AT PARSONS SCHOOL OF DESIGN/SCHOOL OF VISUAL ARTS (12 CLASSES)
8. LOOKING AT PORTFOLIOS (62 TIMES)

THEY SAY THE AVERAGE GRAPHIC DESIGN BOOK SELLS IN THE THOUSANDS WORLDWIDE. IF MORE THAN 10,000 WORLDWIDE ARE SOLD YOU CAN CALL IT A BIG SUCCESS. HOW IS ANYONE MAKING MONEY WITH THESE BOOKS.

WHOM DID WE CALL (EXCLUDING PERSONAL PHONE CALLS):

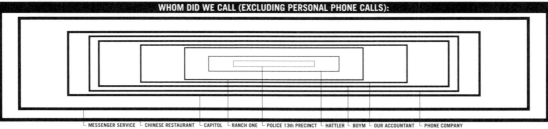

MESSENGER SERVICE | CHINESE RESTAURANT | CAPITOL | RANCH ONE | POLICE 13th PRECINCT | HATTLER | BOYM | OUR ACCOUNTANT | PHONE COMPANY

SOME LINES, HEARD OVER AND OVER AGAIN:

(WORK RELATED)

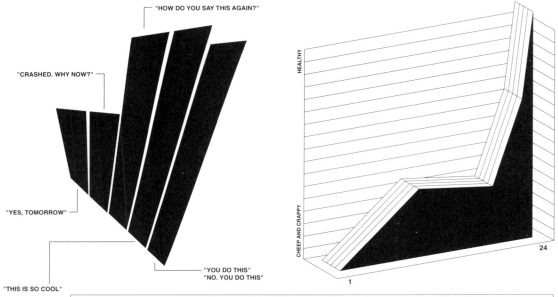

"HOW DO YOU SAY THIS AGAIN?"

"CRASHED. WHY NOW?"

"YES, TOMORROW"

"YOU DO THIS"
"NO. YOU DO THIS"

"THIS IS SO COOL"

OUR EATING HABITS:

HEALTHY

CHEEP AND CRAPPY

1

24

THE 10 WORST THINGS ABOUT HAVING YOUR OWN OFFICE: YOU HAVE TO MAKE ALL DECISIONS; YOU ARE RESPONSIBLE FOR THE DECISIONS (YOU HAVE NO BOSS TO BLAME); YOU CAN'T JUST QUIT; INSTEAD OF ONLY DESIGNING YOU HAVE TO MAKE STUPID PHONE CALLS; ALL THE OTHER DESIGNERS HATE YOU; YOU DRINK A LOT; YOU WORK MANY WEEKENDS; YOU MATURE WITH THE SPEED OF LIGHT; YOU GAIN WEIGHT; YOU'RE SUPPOSED TO BE A MORAL FORCE FOR YOUR EMPLOYEES/INTERNS.

TYPEFACES USED:

DIN

TRADE GOTHIC

HELVETICA

AKZIDENZ GROTESK

VARIOUS

OFFICE PERFORMANCE:

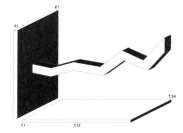

P.1

P.1

T.1   T.12   T.24

TYPEFACES WE WILL NOT USE:

ROTIS, ROTIS SANS, ROTIS SERIF, ROTIS SEMI SANS, ROTIS SEMI SERIF

WEIRDEST TYPEFACE WE EVER USED:

★ CONGO, 1996 (Heinz Schwanziger) ★

THE SCRATCH-OFF GAMES AND HOW MUCH MONEY WE WON:

56 WIN FOR LIFE ($2 ea)	$24
21 TWO FOR ONE ($1 ea)	$ 0
5 SUPERSTAR ($1 ea)	$76
70 TAKE FIVE ($1 ea)	$ 0

PROJECT OVERVIEW

ALL PROJECTS IN THIS BOOK WERE ART DIRECTED AND DESIGNED BY JAN WILKER & HJALTI KARLSSON OF NEW YORK CITY'S KARLSSONWILKER INC. ADDITIONAL DESIGNERS ARE LISTED ACCORDINGLY.

Pages 28 to 29
A CD package for Pat Metheny Trio *Live*
Band photography: Hou Vielz
Client: Warner Bros. Records, CA, 2000
Typeface: Din

Pages 30 to 33
The End Catalog, Missing Monuments /
Buildings of Disaster
Photography of objects: Boym Partners Inc.
Client: Boym Partners Inc., NYC, 2000
Typeface: 3D Type (based on Din)

Pages 34 to 35
Type exploration for SURGE
Client: Landor Associates, NYC, 2000
Typefaces: various

Pages 36 to 39
EL DINER restaurant
Client: Goldman Properties, NYC, 2000
Typeface: karlssonwilker inc.'s El Font

Page 40 (3rd row, left)
Photography: © Spessi

Page 43
CD packaging for Matt Moran, *Sideshow: Songs of Charles Ives*
Client: CRI/Blueshift, NYC, 2000
Photography: Stock
Typeface: Helvetica

Page 44 to 45
Design for a psychology conference
Client: The German Association of Psychology, 2001
Typefaces: Trade Gothic; Akzidenz Grotesk and Dot Matrix (yellow poster)

Pages 46 to 47
Our opening announcement, 2001
Photography: in-house
Typefaces: Din and Trade Gothic

Pages 81 to 85
Various designs for our office, 2001
Typeface: Trade Gothic

Page 86 to 87
Redesign of the lion logo
Client: Anne Klein Group, NYC, 2001

Pages 90 to 91
Identity, ads, and everything else for Stone Street Tavern
Client: Goldman Properties, NYC, 2001
Additional designer: Miriam Wilker
Typefaces: Highway Gothic and Hoefler Text

Pages 92 to 95
CD package for Scott Fields Ensemble, *96 Gestures*
Client: CRI/Blueshift, NYC, 2001
Additional designer: Miriam Wilker
Typeface: Balance

Page 96
A Parasite® business card
Typeface: Trade Gothic

Pages 98 to 99
CD package for John Hollenbeck, *No Images*
Client: CRI/Blueshift, NYC, 2001
Photography: Adobe Photoshop library
Typeface: Franklin Gothic

Pages 100 to 101
CD package and tour poster for Kraan, *Live 2001*
Client: Bassball Records, Germany, 2001
Photography: Eib Eibelshaeuser
Gradation: Adobe Illustrator swatch library
Additional designer: Miriam Wilker
Typeface: Trade Gothic

Pages 102 to 103
Dog lamp
Client: Worldstudio Foundation, NYC, 2001

Pages 104 to 105
CD package for John Hollenbeck, *Quartet Lucy* and *The Claudia Quintet*
Client: CRI/Blueshift, NYC, 2001
Photography: Theo Bleckman (*The Claudia Quintet*)
Additional designer: Cedric Suming
Typeface: Helvetica

Pages 106 to 109
CD package, poster, and TV spot for Moth, *Provisions, Fiction and Gear*
Client: Virgin Records, CA, 2001
Photography (red, yellow, and blue backgrounds on p.106 and backgrounds on p.109): Justin Stephens
Typefaces: various

Page 110
CD package for the 36 Crazyfists, *Bitterness the Star*
Client: Roadrunner Records, NYC, 2001
Photography: Daniel Moss
Typefaces: Akzidenz Grotesk and Andante

Page 111
Press announcements for Skitch Henderson's New York Pops
Client: General Strategic Marketing, NYC, 2001
Photography: Steve J. Sherman
Typeface: Bodoni

Page 112
A super lame pamphlet
Client: Consulate General of Iceland, NYC, 2001
Typeface: Garamond

Page 145
Our website promo, 2001
Typefaces: Din or Trade Gothic

Page 146
Our website, 2001
Flash programming: Francisco Castro
Typefaces: Din or Trade Gothic

Page 147
Project for Staff International
Client: Staff International, NYC, 2001

Page 148 (3rd row, middle)
A sad looking stamp
Client: Kapitola, Iceland, 2001
Font: We forgot

Page 149 (4th row, middle)
Cover for Novum Magazine
Client: Novum Magazine, Germany, 2002
Typefaces: Helvetica and Trade Gothic

Pages 150 to 153
Naming, identity, ads, and everything else for Trust restaurant, Philadelphia
Client: Goldman Properties, NYC, 2001
Photography: Todd Eberle (p.151 top) and stock (acrobats)
Typeface: Akzidenz Grotesk

Pages 154 to 155
Stationary system and various logos for Anne Klein Group and its sublabels.
Client: Anne Klein Group, NYC, 2001
Additional designer (third from top on p.155): Jean Lee
Typefaces: Various

Page 156
Pattern design for AK Anne Klein
Anne Klein Group, NY, 2002

Page 157
Media kit and on-air promos for VH1, NYC, 2001
Photography: Jan Wilker (top) and Matthias Ernstberger (3)
Models: Alastair Bell (guy with cardboard box), Matthias Ernstberger (kneeling naked boy), Vera Yuan (blurry woman), Hjalti Karlsson (crowbar guy), Josandra Armillas (happy woman).
Typeface: Helvetica

Page 158
Our 2001 and 2002 Christmas cards
Typefaces: Din and Charcoal

Page 160
CD package for promo
Client: DreamWorks Records, CA, 2001
Additional designer: Daniel Pepice
Typeface: Akzidenz Grotesk

Page 161
Window display for *Attempts on Her Life*
Client: SoHo Rep, NYC, 2002
Assembling: Jean Lee
Typeface: Helvetica

Pages 164 to 167
CDs, posters, buttons, and everything else for The Vines, *Highly Evolved*
Client: Capitol Records, CA, 2002
Band photography: Daniel Gabbay
Painting (p.167 bottom right): Craig Nicholls
Typefaces: Trade Gothic and Jan's handwriting

Page 168 (4th row, right)
Business card for a lawyer
Typefaces: Caslon and Akzidenz Grotesk

Page 169 (3rd row, right)
T-shirt graphics
Client: Sharksucker, Germany, 2002
Typefaces: Various

Page 169 (4th row, middle)
Logo explorations for Nickelback
Client: Roadrunner Records, NYC, 2001
Typeface: Various

Pages 170 to 171
CD package, single, and tour poster for Hattler; *Mallberry Moon*
Client: Bassball Records/Hattler, Germany, 2002
Photography: Armin Buhl
Typeface: Spartan

Pages 172 to 175
Curious Boym, a book on their studio
Client: Princeton Architectural Press, NY, 2002
Cover photography: Ella Smolarz
Typefaces: Akzidenz Grotesk, Monoline Script, and Tekton

Page 176
Logo for Salgo Medical Center, Munich, Germany, 2002
Client: Gabor Salgo
Typeface: We forgot

Page 193
CD and tour poster for Hattler; *No Eats Yes*
Client: Universal Music/Polydor, Germany, 2000
Photography: Jan Wilker
Typeface: Spartan

Pages 194 to 195
Hattler remix CDs
Client: Bassball Records, 2002 (p.194) and M10, France, 2002 (p.195)
Typeface: Spartan

Page 197
Design for a line of cosmetics
Client: Marie - Laurence LLC., NY, 2002
Horse illustration: Sabina Hahn
Typefaces: Highway Gothic and something else

Page 198
The original tape of The SPOKEN PORTFOLIO®.
Typeface: Jan's handwriting

Page 199
Our second mailer
Typefaces: Trade Gothic and Din

Pages 204 to 205
CD packaging for Skúli Sverrisson/Óskar Gudjónsson, *After Silence*
Client: Edda Publishing, Iceland, 2002
Photography: Skúli's and Óskar's family members
Typeface: Times New Roman (the Icelandic cut)

Pages 206 to 208
CD package for Elemental Chill
Client: Kriztal Entertainment, MI, 2002
Typefaces: Subcaps and Din

Page 222 (top row, right)
Short movie, 2.30 minutes, stop motion
Client: karlssonwilker inc.
Model: Joerg Globas

Page 223 (top row, middle)
Our second mailer
Typefaces: Din and Trade Gothic

Page 223 (2nd row, right)
Business card for Nexus architects
Client: Nexus architects, Iceland, 2001
Typefaces: We forgot

Page 224 (top row, right)
The Op-Art page from *Graphis* magazine
Client: *Graphis* Magazine, NYC, 2002
Typefaces: Din and Trade Gothic

Page 224 (3rd row, left)
A page from Form Magazine
Client: Form Magazine, Germany, 2002
Fonts: Din and Trade Gothic

THE GETTING-ALL-EXCITED PLANT

(WORK RELATED)

Virgin calls for our portfolio: a possible project with Spike Jonze. According to the people at Virgin, Mr. Spike looks at a bunch of portfolios, and then returns all of them except ours, which he keeps for a few weeks. —We do not get the job.

Warner Bros. calls. We will work on the new Red Hot Chili Pepper package with the artist Julian Schnabel. —In the end Mr. Schnabel does the whole thing all by himself.

There is a possibility that we will work on a full-blown branding project for a huge trucking company (they have 15 12-wheel trucks). —We are still waiting to start.

A guy from a film production company asks us if we're interested in directing. —And somehow it all evaporates.

AGI records calls in for our book for a possible CD package for Beck. We are huge fans. We keep our fingers crossed for a few weeks. —Nothing.

A Boston ad agency leaves a message on our machine, a job for TCM. We don't check the messages until the following day. —They never return our calls.

An ad agency calls in for our portfolio: to art direct the 10th-anniversary issue of Big magazine. —In the end another studio does the job.

We and three other design studios work on a paid pitch for VH1. —In the end they select another design company to do the project.

We needed some time to get accustomed to the the fact that not all leads turn into jobs. So we trained ourselves not to get completely excited about potential projects, but it still never really works.

THE 11 BEST THINGS ABOUT HAVING YOUR OWN OFFICE:

(BASED SOLELY ON OUR EXPERIENCE DURING THE FIRST 2 YEARS IN BUSINESS)

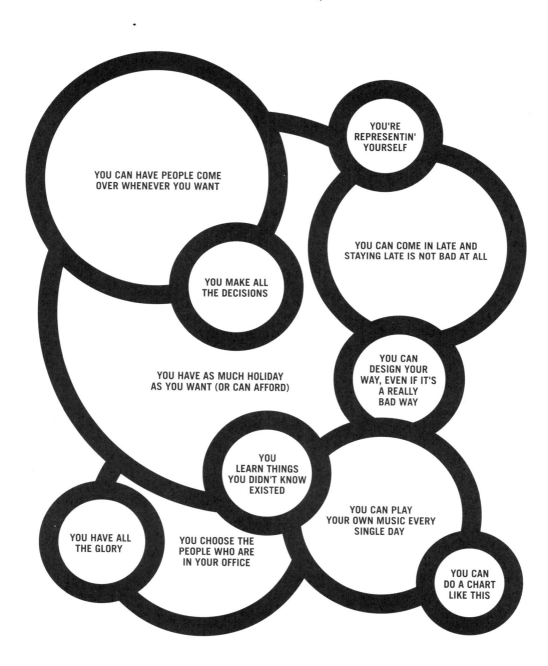

THAT'S IT FOR NOW
AND THANK YOU FOR FLIPPING THROUGH THIS BOOK

GOOD